# pink floyd
## behind the music

# pink floyd
## behind the music

## mike evans

**G:**

**G:**

First published in the UK in 2025
by Gemini Books
Part of Gemini Books Group

Based in Woodbridge and London

Marine House, Tide Mill Way,
Woodbridge, Suffolk, IP12 1AP,
United Kingdom

www.geminibooks.com

ISBN 9781786751560

A CIP catalogue record for this book is available from the British Library.

Bound and printed in China
10 9 8 7 6 5 4 3 2 1

Page 2: Pink Floyd, 2005

# contents

# introduction

ABOVE LEFT: Pink Floyd concert ticket for Wembley Stadium, London, August 5, 1988

ABOVE RIGHT: Guitarist and lead singer Syd Barrett performing live with Pink Floyd, 1967

OPPOSITE: Bassist Roger Waters, 1977

**P**ioneers of what was once dubbed "progressive rock" with their extended songs, technical experimentation, challenging lyrics, and spectacular stage presentations, Pink Floyd have been hailed as one of the most influential bands in the last half century of popular music. And unlike most bands of the progressive persuasion, the group has endured in the public consciousness, via a string of iconic recordings now regarded as timeless classics.

Originally formed in the mid-1960s as a typical British rhythm and blues group, the four-piece—vocalist/guitarist Syd Barrett, bass guitarist Roger Waters, Rick Wright on keyboards, and drummer Nick Mason—quickly evolved into one of the pioneers of psychedelic rock. Under the tacit leadership of chief songwriter Barrett, with two hit singles and the ground-breaking album *The Piper at the Gates of Dawn*, they defined the "flower power" music of 1967, complete with hallucinogenic lyrics, distorted guitar effects, and an innovative light show. Syd's days as the main creative force were numbered, however, as his drug dependency led to his replacement by guitarist David Gilmour early in 1968.

This was the line-up that would persist through most of the band's career, with *A Saucerful of Secrets*, *Ummagumma*, and *Atom Heart Mother* hugely successful in the charts by the early 1970s, though deemed "uncommercial" in their experimental approach to both recording and songwriting. By the time *Meddle* was released in 1971, however, Roger Waters would dominate the composer credits on the album, with all but one of its seven tracks either written or co-written by the bass guitarist. And on the same release, Gilmour took the majority of lead vocals. There was a distinct division of labor emerging, with Mason and Wright taking a more supporting role in the scheme of things. This would have profound effects in the subsequent evolution of the group.

Through 1972, Pink Floyd perfected what would prove to be an artistic and commercial triumph when, between extensive touring, they put together the material for *The Dark Side of the Moon*. Using the latest in recording technology, the concept album—with lyrics exclusively by Waters—addressed daunting themes such as death, greed, and mental illness. On its release in March 1973, it became an instant classic, selling more than forty-five million copies worldwide.

Waters' vision was dominant again in 1975 with the critically acclaimed *Wish You Were Here*, inspired by bouts of nostalgia regarding the departure of Syd Barrett, and an obsessive skepticism about the music business. The album, another chart-topper on both sides of the Atlantic, was followed in 1976 by *Animals*, in which various tensions within the band, particularly between Gilmour and Waters, came to a head.

The central issue was over the division of royalties, with an underlying concern over the basic dynamic of the group, and Waters' increasing dominance in all they did. And commercial success brought more problems. On the American tour promoting *Animals*, the band played huge stadiums for the first time, to which Waters, in particular, found it hard to adjust. So

fraught was the atmosphere on the road that at one stage Rick Wright actually threatened to quit.

Faced with financial ruin due to fiscal mismanagement, in 1979 the band's fortunes were rescued by another bold concept for an album, again courtesy of Roger Waters. *The Wall*, with its central character loosely based on Syd Barrett and Waters himself, pictured a washed-up rock star who builds a figurative "wall" between himself and society at large.

Once again Waters' personal frustrations dominated the subject matter, and despite the superb musicianship of all the members concerned, stresses within the ranks were such that Wright was fired before the album was completed. Nevertheless, *The Wall*, and its spin-off hit single, "Another Brick in the Wall (Part 2)," represented another huge success, and another marker in Roger Waters' seemingly unstoppable takeover of the group's creative output.

The next Pink Floyd album, 1983's *The Final Cut*, was judged by at least one critic as basically a Roger Waters solo collection. Waters and Gilmour were working increasingly independently of each other, with fractures in the band widening as both the bass player and guitarist released their own albums. And by 1984, the break-up of Pink Floyd seemed inevitable. However, after much legal wrangling, it was Waters who left the group, leaving Dave Gilmour and Nick Mason to head the next Floyd release, *A Momentary Lapse of Reason*, in 1987.

Mason and Gilmour reunited with Rick Wright for their 1994

album, *The Division Bell*. And although the three got together with Roger Waters for the Live 8 charity concert in 2005, Rick Wright's tragic death in 2008 put an end to any speculation as to further reunions of the full personnel. As a tribute to Wright's memory, however, in 2014 Mason and Gilmour revisited tracks recorded with Wright during the *Division Bell* sessions, to create a new album, *The Endless River*. And in 2022, Gilmour and Mason got together once more as Pink Floyd to record the single "Hey, Hey, Rise Up!" raising funds for the people of Ukraine after the Russian invasion. It may well have been the final musical gesture under the banner of Pink Floyd.

With their pioneering use of studio technology (at a time when synthesizers and quadraphonic sound were in their infancy), extended compositions that broke away from conventional rock song structures, and the ambitious themes and concepts characterizing their material, Pink Floyd have genuinely expanded the landscape of rock music forever. Among generations of musicians citing the band as a key influence, we can name David Bowie, Queen, and Radiohead as just a brief sample.

The legacy of Pink Floyd lies in their recorded work, with their albums, as related in these pages, marking key milestones in their extraordinary history. It's a history of a band—not without its own internal discord and division—molded by the vision of its various members, with each album representing something genuinely unique to British rock music.

OPPOSITE: *Pink Floyd: The Wall* movie poster, 1982

ABOVE: Pink Floyd, July 2, 2005. L-R: Nick Mason, David Gilmour, Rick Wright, and Roger Waters pose for a studio portrait backstage at Live 8 London, Hyde Park.

PAGES 12-13: Pink Floyd performing at Bristol University, UK, March 3, 1969

# the piper at the gates of dawn

"You have to be careful when you start on this psychedelic thing. We don't call ourselves a psychedelic group or say that we play psychedelic pop music."

**Nick Mason**

The "14 Hour Technicolor Dream," staged on April 29, 1967, was the brainchild of a group of movers and shakers on the London counterculture stage. In the spirit of the now-legendary "gathering of the tribes," the "Human Be-In" that had been staged in San Francisco in mid-January, the event was a spectacular evocation of the hallucinogenic experience of mind-altering drugs, even for those who didn't actually indulge at the time. As a review in *Melody Maker* put it: "It was the first serious attempt at a 'Human Be-In' in England, therefore an attempt to bring forth some of the ideals of the underground movement."

Organized as a benefit for the *International Times* magazine, the all-night hippie extravaganza at the imposing Victorian Alexandra Palace in the north of the capital featured some of the leading lights of the nascent underground, heralding the dawn of the much-publicized Summer of Love later that same year.

There were two stages at either end of the enormous hall, with a gantry halfway between from which the sound and lights were controlled. Bands were playing simultaneously, so as members of the audience wandered from one end to the other, they would experience the sound of one group morphing into the

OPPOSITE: Roger Waters performs live onstage with Pink Floyd at the Architectural Association student party, London, December 16, 1966

ABOVE: Pink Floyd pose for a portrait in 1967, London, UK

sound of the other. There were fairground rides and inflatables, experimental movies and abstract images projected on the walls—an all-in sensory happening, the like of which had never been seen on such a scale in the UK, attended by an estimated ten thousand revelers.

Record producer Joe Boyd would recall in his 1960s memoir *White Bicycles*: "I don't think much money was made, but none was lost, and the event got huge publicity plus royal visits from Lennon and Hendrix . . . There was no stopping this juggernaut; the Underground was becoming the mainstream."

As well as over two dozen cutting-edge bands—including The Crazy World of Arthur Brown, Soft Machine, The Move, and The Pretty Things—there were innovative light shows, and an array of left-field acts such as The Exploding Galaxy dance troupe, poets Michael Horovitz and Christopher Logue, and the relatively unknown conceptual artist Yoko Ono.

And top of the bill were the current favorites of the emerging "psychedelic" music scene, Pink Floyd. The group had just released their debut single, "Arnold Layne," in early March, and were in the middle of recording their first album, *The Piper at the Gates of Dawn*, which would make the Top Ten in the UK album charts when it appeared in August.

Although details differ in various accounts, Pink Floyd had first played under that name (initially as The Pink Floyd Sound) in 1965, and prior to that under a variety of short-lived titles (with ever-changing line-ups) including Sigma 6, The Screaming Abdabs, and The Megadeaths. Three of the four key members— bass player Roger Waters, keyboard man Richard Wright, and drummer Nick Mason—had first met as fellow architecture students at the Regent Street Polytechnic in central London, before recruiting guitarist/vocalist Syd Barrett in 1964.

## Cambridge

Roger Waters was born in Great Bookham, Surrey, on September 6, 1943. Radical political credentials ran through his veins, with his father, Eric (the son of a coal miner), a militant Christian socialist, and for a time a card-carrying member of the Communist Party. Upon Eric Waters' death— killed on military service in February 1944, at the Battle of Anzio in Italy—Roger's mother, Mary, relocated to Cambridge, where the future rock star would spend his childhood and formative teen years. And it was in Cambridge that Roger Waters crossed paths with future Pink Floyd luminaries Syd Barrett and David Gilmour for the first time.

Alongside a decidedly anti-authoritarian streak—during his mid-teens he was a leading light in the local youth branch of CND (the Campaign for Nuclear Disarmament) protesting against nuclear weapons—Roger's passion was music. But although rock 'n' roll had burst onto the scene in 1955–56,

when kids of his age were its target audience, initially Roger's musical enthusiasm was for "trad" jazz and vintage blues. It was following the impact of The Beatles and The Rolling Stones in the early part of the 1960s, by which time he had left Cambridge for college life in London, that Roger began to be influenced by what was happening on the contemporary UK music scene.

More than two years his junior, Syd Barrett had attended the same primary and secondary schools as Waters, namely Morley Memorial Primary (where Roger's mother taught Barrett briefly) and the Cambridgeshire High School for Boys. Syd, whose real name was Roger Keith Barrett, was born on January 6, 1946, and from an early age showed creative leanings. As well as a talent for visual art, he was also demonstrably musical, having played ukulele, followed by banjo and guitar, from the age of ten. After his time at Cambridgeshire High, where he had made the acquaintance of Roger Waters, in September 1962 he gained a place in the art department of the local "tech" school, Cambridgeshire College of Arts and Technology, studying art and design. It was here that he would practice regularly in

lunch hours with guitarist David Gilmour, although the two had first met when Gilmour was at the (more exclusive, fee-paying) Perse School, just down the road from Cambridgeshire High. But although art was assumed to be Barrett's prime conviction, from the early months of 1962 music was increasingly his main focus.

One of Barrett's first ventures in playing with an actual group had been in 1962 when he teamed up with aspiring vocalist Geoff Mottlow, as guitarist in Geoff Mott and the Mottoes. Specializing in covers of late-fifties rock hits, they rehearsed in Syd's home, but played few paying gigs. (It has to be remembered, of course, that in the earliest stages of their careers even The Beatles and Stones were essentially "covers bands," with repertoires that were 90 percent American, be it classic rock 'n' roll, rhythm and blues, or early-sixties soul.) Roger Waters was also known to play bass with the Mottoes on the odd occasion.

Another brief flirtation on Syd's part was with The Hollerin' Blues, a short-lived outfit led by his guitarist friend, also studying at the art college, John Gordon. And by 1963 Barrett had landed himself a further band gig, this time with Those Without, yet another obscure name on the somewhat incestuous roster of Cambridge-based bands of the era.

## London

Roger Waters, meanwhile, had made the break from the Cambridge scene when he was offered a place in the School of Architecture at Regent Street Polytechnic in the autumn of 1962. Just a minute's walk from the BBC's Broadcasting House, and less than five minutes from the Marquee Club in Oxford Street (where history was being made as the hub of the burgeoning UK R&B scene), the Poly couldn't have been more central to where the action was, as far as Waters was concerned.

He'd dabbled with music in Cambridge, of course—including his short tenure

Syd Barrett (above left), drummer Nick Mason (above right), and keyboardist Rick Wright (opposite) at London's UFO club, circa 1967

ABOVE: A psychedelic light show surrounds Pink Floyd as they perform live onstage at the Architectural Association student party, London, December 16, 1966

as bass player with Geoff Mott's Mottoes—but in the main had preferred to hone his skills on the bass guitar in private. All that was to change, however, when he moved to London, and into the orbit of similar-minded students, whose ambitions were more musical than architectural.

Unlike Waters, drummer Nick Mason had caught the rock 'n' roll bug, when as a twelve-year-old schoolboy in 1956, he bought Bill Haley's "See You Later, Alligator" on a shellac 78 disc. Born in Birmingham on January 27, 1944, Mason grew up in Hampstead, London, where after acquiring a drum kit in his early teens he played in his first group, The Hotrods, formed with some school friends. As Mason would admit, the band never really got beyond playing (or at least attempting to play) the theme from the TV series *Peter Gunn*.

At secondary school, an independent boarding establishment called Frensham Heights, he also developed a liking for jazz (first traditional or "trad" jazz, then bebop, which at the time was categorized as "modern" jazz). But the sheer technical challenge of bebop put him off developing in that direction: "As a teenager, the advanced playing techniques required were an insurmountable barrier. I went back to perfecting the drum part to 'Peter Gunn.'"

As soon as he enrolled in the architecture department at Regent Street Poly, Mason soon struck up a friendship with Roger Waters, despite the latter's seemingly aloof attitude. As well as the college assignments they teamed up on, they had shared interests—in vintage cars (after Roger had unsuccessfully asked to borrow Nick's 1930 Austin "Chummy"), and of course, music. Waters would be seen wandering the corridors between lectures, guitar in hand, heading for a space where he might practice—and more often than not with his new-found drummer friend.

Things moved on a stage in early 1963 when Roger and Nick read a message on the college noticeboard, asking if anyone was interested in forming a group. The notice had been placed by two students who had already been playing casual gigs as a duo, vocalist Keith Noble and bass guitarist Clive Metcalfe. Rehearsing in the student common room, or the tearoom in the basement of the college, Noble and Metcalfe took Mason and Waters on board, with the latter playing a lead guitar role. The line-up expanded to a quintet with the addition of Keith's sister Sheilagh as an occasional second vocalist, then to a sextet with the involvement of keyboard player Richard Wright. With Wright's girlfriend Juliette taking over from Sheilagh Noble as vocalist, they now dubbed themselves Sigma 6, playing mainly student hops and private parties. But more significantly, the presence together of Roger Waters, Nick Mason, and now Richard Wright, represented the earliest genesis of what would become Pink Floyd.

Richard Wright, or Rick Wright as he was more often referred to, was born in Hatch End, a north-western suburb of London, on July 28, 1943. Educated privately at the Haberdashers' Aske's school, he was something of a musical prodigy, having taught himself the rudiments of guitar, trumpet, trombone, and piano before hitting his teens. Like many of his generation, his first interest was skiffle and trad jazz rather than the increasingly anodyne music gracing the pop charts in the late 1950s, and from there his ever-broadening taste took in the more complex modern jazz of musicians like Miles Davis and John Coltrane.

Without a keyboard set-up of his own, Wright's public appearances with Sigma 6—and their subsequent brief manifestations as The Abdabs, The Screaming Abdabs, and The Megadeaths—were limited to venues where there was a piano available. Nevertheless, even after quitting the course after a year, and traveling to Greece before enrolling at the Royal College of Music, Rick remained in close contact with Roger and Nick.

## Leonard's Lodgers

At the beginning of Waters and Mason's second year at the Poly, in September 1963, Noble and Metcalfe decided to revert to their previous configuration as a duo, terminating once and for all the brief lifespan of Sigma 6. Now without a semblance of a band, Roger and Nick were also at a loose end regarding London accommodation as the new term began, when to the rescue came Mike Leonard.

Leonard was a part-time lecturer on the architecture course at the Poly, and was also teaching at Hornsey College of Art. As well as architecture, Leonard's enthusiasms embraced the relationship between rhythm, sound, and light. At the rambling house he had recently bought in Highgate, north London, he indulged in experiments with light machines and such; but he needed some rental tenants to offset the overheads of his otherwise expensive property.

Nick and Roger were the first in what proved to be an illustrious list of tenants at 39 Stanhope Gardens. The pair rented the large flat on the ground floor, which under their tenure also doubled as a rehearsal space, with Mike Leonard living above them. For the two students, now far more committed to music than architecture, it was an ideal situation, even though one of their tutors was involved in the set-up. And Mike had his own musical agenda, playing keyboards (a Farfisa electric

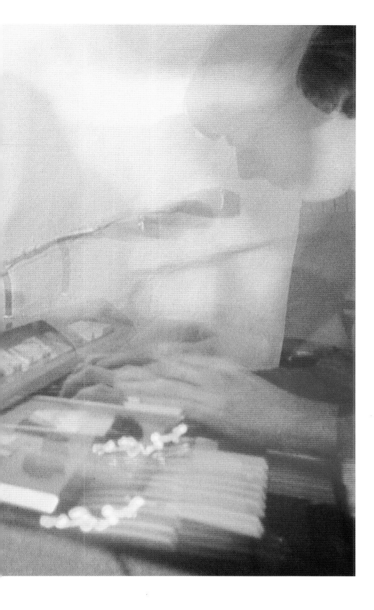

a few casual gigs with the line-up, before being succeeded by Syd Barrett.

Already known to Roger Waters from the Cambridge scene, Barrett had moved down to London with Bob Klose, after gaining a place at Camberwell College of Art. And it wasn't long before Syd had moved into the creative community at Stanhope Gardens, as had Rick Wright and his girlfriend Juliette Gale. Syd's place in the line-up was virtually settled by default when, soon after he appeared on the scene, the RAF decided to transfer Chris Dennis to a post in Bahrain.

The band's repertoire was the standard, and at the time very fashionable, American R&B. Spearheaded by groups like The Rolling Stones and The Yardbirds, what had attracted a cult following at the weekly rhythm and blues sessions at the Marquee back in 1962 was now a full-blown national trend, with hit records to prove it. The band's appearances, mainly at student dances at the Polytechnic, relied on covering songs by Bo Diddley, The Rolling Stones, and similar material. Syd Barrett—who, contrary to the view of most R&B devotees, also confessed to preferring The Beatles to the Stones—had yet to reveal himself as a songwriter.

It was during Chris Dennis's short membership of the band that the name Pink Floyd was first coined, after being suggested by Syd Barrett. Barrett had already named his two pet cats Pink and Floyd, after two relatively obscure American blues musicians, Pink Anderson and Floyd Council. Occasionally calling themselves The Tea Set, until they discovered another outfit had already adopted that moniker, Pink Floyd (initially The Pink Floyd Sound) was the one that stuck.

Around Christmas 1964, Syd made his earliest "professional" venture into songwriting when the band made their first demo recordings. The sessions, which Nick Mason recalls cost the group nothing, were courtesy of a friend of Rick Wright who worked in a studio in West Hampstead. As well as the R&B classic "I'm a King Bee"—a Slim Harpo original from 1957 which had recently appeared on The Rolling Stones' debut album—the recordings included four numbers penned by Barrett and one by Roger Waters. Syd's songs were "Double O Bo" (referencing the James Bond theme and Bo Diddley), "Lucy Leave," "Remember Me," and "Butterfly." The Roger Waters original was "Walk with Me Sydney," which featured Rick's girlfriend Juliette Gale sharing the lead vocals with Syd. The tracks would not see the light of day commercially until 2015, when they appeared on the vinyl-only release *1965: Their First Recordings*.

Early in 1965, with Bob Klose still in the line-up, the band secured a regular gig at the Countdown Club in the affluent west London area of Kensington. Inside, the basement cellar was far from affluent looking, with minimal decor and a small bar. It was a baptism of fire for the group, playing three ninety-minute sets between nine at night and two or three in the morning. By

organ), albeit with no ambitions further than jamming with Mason and Waters—especially when Rick Wright resumed rehearsing with the pair on a regular basis.

In the late summer of 1964, Nick Mason decided that the distractions at Stanhope Gardens were making studying virtually impossible, so he decided to relocate back home in Hampstead. His place in the flatshare with Roger Waters was taken by a new student on the Poly architecture course, and another ex-pupil of Cambridgeshire High School, Bob Klose. A more than competent guitarist, Klose added a layer of expertise to the proceedings when it came to jamming in Mike Leonard's front room.

The embryonic group, dubbing themselves Leonard's Lodgers in deference to their keyboard-playing landlord, soon realized that what was missing now was a vocalist. To that end Klose brought in another ex-Cambridge character, at the time a dental assistant in the RAF, Chris Dennis. Dennis—whose main attraction for the others was that he owned a fully functioning PA system—lasted

*The Lord of the Rings* and *The Wind in the Willows*, delivered in a uniquely "English" accent. All of the band were familiar with drugs, of course—cannabis, various amphetamines, and the increasingly available "acid" (lysergic acid diethylamide or LSD)—but Barrett was already veering toward over-indulgence, especially in the case of acid. And there was an edge to his songwriting that certainly reflected this.

## Psychedelia

Although their gigs were still few and far between, the band's onstage image was also developing in directions outside the expectations of a regular R&B audience. Roger Waters in particular had been fascinated by the light-and-sound experiments conducted by Mike Leonard at Stanhope Gardens, and in Mike's studio workshop at Hornsey College of Art. The "light machines," projecting abstract patterns on a wall by means of perforated discs rotated by electric motors, were prototypes of what would be *de règle* for any self-respecting psychedelic band by 1967.

In his personal account of the band's history, Nick Mason recalls that a key appearance in March 1966 was at the Rag Ball, at Essex University in Colchester. For their set, Mason describes how "someone had arranged oil slides and a film projection," linking it directly to the next big event in the group's career: "I imagine that someone there or subsequent word of mouth was responsible for leading us on to the Marquee."

However tenuous the link with the Essex Rag Ball, Pink Floyd were booked for a series of Sunday afternoon "happenings" at the Marquee Club, dubbed the Spontaneous Underground. The mixed-media events had been set up by a cohort of influential characters on the London countercultural scene a few weeks earlier. Pink Floyd's somewhat anarchic approach to playing rock/blues at this stage made them an ideal "house band" for the weekly gatherings, which featured free-form jazz, poetry readings, avant-garde theater, and often included the

the beginning of the third set they had invariably run out of numbers, but soon realized that to avoid repetition they could string out numbers with longer improvised solos—an early portent of things to come.

When Bob Klose decided to leave the band in July of 1965, after much pressure from his parents and college tutors who felt his studies were being neglected, Syd Barrett again assumed a front-line role by default, this time as lead guitarist as well as vocalist. By this time Syd, Rick Wright, and Roger Waters had already begun experimenting with guitar distortion, electronic feedback, and so on, and Klose's departure signaled a further move away from the blues-based sound that had been the band's signature style up until then.

Now, with Syd's songs also an increasing feature of their repertoire, an original Pink Floyd sound was beginning to emerge. From the start, Syd's compositions featured distinctive, often whimsical lyrics, influenced by a variety of sources that included

improvisational musical ensemble AMM.

Keith Rowe, the AMM guitarist, made a particular impression on Syd Barrett when both outfits played at the same event. As described by writer (and counterculture activist at the time) Barry Miles, "Two of Barrett's signature guitar techniques were taken from Keith Rowe. The use of ball bearings, rolled down the strings, and the detuning of the strings as a musical effect during a solo . . ." It was also at one of the Spontaneous Underground afternoons at the Marquee that Pink Floyd would meet their future manager Peter Jenner for the first time.

A lecturer at the London School of Economics, Peter Jenner was one of the participants in the London Free School, an anarchist-leaning cooperative of like-minded creative folk and underground activists. The LFS was founded by John "Hoppy" Hopkins, and alongside Jenner, other major backers included Joe Boyd, a young American who ran the UK arm of Elektra Records, and Barry Miles (aka "Miles"). Jenner, Hopkins, and others had set up DNA, an independent record label dedicated to experimental and free-form music, and recorded the AMM improvisers. But Jenner soon realized that to make any real money, the label needed what he described as a "pop band."

It was at that point that Jenner came across the embryonic Pink Floyd, at a Spontaneous Underground event at the Marquee. Although the band were still playing standard R&B numbers as their basic set—plus Barrett's idiosyncratic songs—he was instantly impressed by what he would describe as the "weird noises" they were achieving instrumentally, instead of the usual bluesy (and, more often than not, predictable) guitar solos. This, he decided, was what he was looking

OPPOSITE: British political activist and journalist John "Hoppy" Hopkins (1937-2015), pictured in 1967

ABOVE: A psychedelic light show illuminates two women dancing in front of the stage while Pink Floyd perform at the UFO Club, London, December 23, 1966

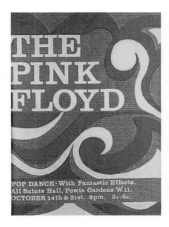

for. It was early summer 1966, and the next time Jenner was in touch with the group was when they reconvened in September—still adhering to a college-driven timetable—after their summer break. At the outset Roger Waters made it clear that what the band needed wasn't a deal with the DNA label, but a manager. Peter agreed almost immediately, offering to look after the band in partnership with an old friend, another co-founder of DNA, Andrew King.

Jenner and King had known each other since their schooldays, and were both at something of a loose end career-wise when the idea of managing a band reared its head. Neither had any experience in the music business, but shared an enthusiasm for jazz, blues, and the more experimental end of rock music. And, key to the Floyd's immediate needs, they had access to a certain amount of capital. Realizing that DNA wasn't working out, the pair wound up the label, and kitted the band out with some much-needed new equipment, including a full PA set-up. They also formed a management company, Blackhill Enterprises—which would incorporate the members of the band in a six-man partnership—and set about putting the name Pink Floyd on the London cultural map.

Along with Jenner, Andrew King was also involved in the London Free School, which was (not surprisingly) in need of finance to survive, and so the pair decided to stage a benefit event on behalf of the LFS. Held at the All Saints Church Hall in Powis Gardens, Notting Hill at the end of September, the gig was the first in a series of fundraisers at the venue, billed variously as a "Pop Dance," "Psychedelic Pop," and "Sound/Light Workshop," and all featuring Pink Floyd. The band played ten All Saints dates over a couple of months, and interspersed with some much-needed paid gigs, by the end of the year they had become established as *the* rock group on the emergent "psychedelic" scene.

Key to the new counterculture in the UK was *International Times* (generally referred to by its initials as *IT*), a fortnightly paper founded by the same LFS movers and shakers (Hoppy, Miles, and co.) that was launched on October 15, 1966. The launch party was another milestone in the genesis of Pink Floyd, with

ABOVE LEFT: A promotional poster designed by Wendy Gair advertising Pink Floyd's All Saints Hall residency, in London, 1966

OPPOSITE: The poster promoting the "14 Hour Technicolor Dream" with Pink Floyd top of the bill

ABOVE RIGHT: A young woman in the audience is projected with Pink Floyd's psychedelic light show at the UFO Club, London, December 1966 the "First All-Night Rave Pop Op Costume Masque Drag Ball Et Al," as it was billed, featuring them as headliners alongside their fellow psychedelic flagbearers, Soft Machine. An all-star turn-out included Paul McCartney, the iconic film actress Monica Vitti, her most celebrated director Michelangelo Antonioni, and (dressed as a sexy nun) Marianne Faithfull. As the *IT* described in a subsequent account of the evening: "The Pink Floyd, psychedelic pop group, did weird things to the feel of the event with their scary feedback sounds, slide projections playing on their skin (drops of paint run riot on the slides to produce outer space/prehistoric textures on the skin), spotlights flashing on them in time with a drum beat . . ."

Netting a string of regular evening sessions (as opposed to the Sunday afternoon happenings) at the Marquee Club, the band was prominent enough to be interviewed by *Melody Maker* in January 1967, and Nick Mason was keen to put the psychedelic label into context: "You have to be careful when you start on this psychedelic thing. We don't call ourselves a psychedelic group or say that we play psychedelic pop music. It's just that people associate us with this and we get employed all the time at the various freak-outs and happenings in London."

Crucial in this burgeoning psychedelic movement was a venue that opened on December 23, 1966—the night after Pink Floyd had commenced their Marquee evening residency—with the band as its flagship attraction. The essence of the psychedelic "experience" was to recreate as far as possible the effects of an hallucinogenic LSD-induced trip. With this in mind, UFO (pronounced you-fo, and short for Underground Freak Out) was established by LFS luminaries "Hoppy" Hopkins and Joe Boyd, who felt the scene needed its own club rather than relying on established venues like the Marquee.

The pair found a location in unlikely premises occupied by an Irish dance hall, the Blarney Club, in Tottenham Court Road. Located under two cinemas, the Friday night sessions couldn't begin until after 10 pm or so, and lasted until dawn. Joe Boyd would recall how a word-of-mouth buzz guaranteed a huge turn-out by the underground community from the word go: "We had no idea who would turn up that first night . . . but freaks came out of the woodwork from all over the city and we made a profit. There was a general feeling of surprise and recognition; few had any idea there were so many kindred spirits."

Pink Floyd, along with Soft Machine, quickly established themselves as the UFO "house bands," both outfits now working with their own lightshows. Added to the trippy atmosphere were the club's own visual effects, which also included old black-and-white movies and screening experimental films between the live bands.

As Barry Miles would write: "UFO was to the Floyd as the

Cavern was to the Beatles. They were unknown when it started and famous when it closed, less than a year later." In its original location at the Blarney Club, UFO ran for just nine months until the end of July 1967, by which time the media-driven fashion for all things psychedelic had captured the public imagination as the "Summer of Love." And Pink Floyd's fortunes were central to the emerging mood, as they burst onto the recording scene with two chart-bound singles before the release of their debut album.

## Single Success

As in many accounts of wheeling and dealing in the 1960s music business, Pink Floyd's initial road to recording success was not without a few bumps on the way. With his connections at the American label Elektra—and experience in actual record production—Joe Boyd seemed a natural choice to engineer a

## "UFO was to the Floyd as the Cavern was to the Beatles. They were unknown when it started and famous when it closed, less than a year later."

## Barry Miles

record deal. When an offer from Elektra was deemed by all as unsatisfactory, Boyd went elsewhere and came up with a far better proposition with Polydor Records, and a session was set up at Sound Techniques in Chelsea. Pink Floyd were on their way.

With Boyd at the production desk, five songs were taped on January 29, 1967 and over the following couple of days, including "Arnold Layne," which would become the A-side of Pink Floyd's debut single. Joe Boyd's position as the band's main man record-wise was cut short, however, when

a booking agent by the name of Bryan Morrison entered the picture. Morrison's agency had booked Pink Floyd for some gigs, and he turned up at the studio, suggesting he could get them a better deal than the Polydor offer, with the all-powerful EMI.

Boyd was subsequently sidelined, although his recording of "Arnold Layne" and its flipside, "Candy and a Currant Bun," would be used on the first EMI Columbia release by the band. The A-side, accompanied by a black-and-white promotional film (before the days of the obligatory promo video) featuring the band frolicking around on a deserted beach, was an early example of the "psychedelic" pop that was beginning to appear in the singles chart.

With what was then the band's trademark sound—Rick Wright's Farfisa organ and Syd Barrett's reverb-heavy guitar to the fore—Barrett's decidedly offbeat lyrics were inspired by a Cambridge cross-dresser, notorious at the time for stealing women's underwear from washing lines!

The flipside, something of a Syd Barrett drug confessional, was originally called "Let's Roll Another One" until the record company objected. Instead, a line "I'm high, don't try to spoil my fun" was deleted from the lyric, and the title changed to "Candy and a Currant Bun." The changes lessened the chance of the single being banned by the BBC (although a couple of pirate stations did put an embargo on it), and it managed to nudge into the Top Twenty chart at No. 20. Released in early March, it would be the only record by the band on which they were credited as *The* Pink Floyd.

Meanwhile, Pink Floyd's gig diary was fuller than ever—aided in no small way by their relationship with the Bryan Morrison agency. Venues ranged from traditional dance halls and civic centers to colleges and universities, and dedicated rock places like the Marquee, Eel Pie Island, and UFO. Plus, there were one-off specials, none more memorable than the "14 Hour Technicolor Dream" with Pink Floyd top of the bill.

During the evening of the *International Times*-sponsored all-nighter, the band had been appearing on a TV show in the Netherlands, *Fan Club*, so arrived at the venue as dawn was breaking. Accounts vary as to the quality of the band's performance, although in the context of the event it was undoubtedly spectacular. As one eyewitness described it: "Their music was eerie and full of odd sounds that seemed to spread uncannily over the gardens and surrounding hills. They hit full orbital momentum as the first rays of the sun entered the enormous rose window, and the people in the crowds throughout the immense hall held hands with their neighbours."

Most observers agreed, however, that Syd Barrett was, to put it mildly, "out of it"—tripping on acid, to the point where his contribution to the music was irrelevant to what else was happening onstage. It was a situation not unique to that particular gig, which would fashion the future of the band—now in the midst of recording their first album—over the coming months.

Just a couple of weeks after the "Technicolor Dream," on May 12, another gig would mark a more significant milestone in the formative history of the band. Deciding to present Pink Floyd in a concert hall venue rather than a club or dance hall, Jenner and King managed to hire the prestigious Queen Elizabeth Hall on London's South Bank. The idea was that a strictly "listening" environment, more often suited to classical recitals, would allow the group to indulge and develop more fully the sound and visual innovations they had been experimenting with in their night-to-night gigs, and latterly the recording studio.

Dubbed "Games for May," the show featured just the band without any support act, for a full two-hour concert. The seated audience were treated to a mixed-media performance that involved a more ambitious lightshow than usual, a bubble machine, and a sound device called the Azimuth Co-ordinator. The latter contraption (state-of-the-art at the time) enabled its operator—in this case Rick Wright—to send the music from his keyboard, plus pre-taped sound effects, to various speakers mounted around the auditorium. It was, in effect, the first quadraphonic sound system. The performance, which *IT* magazine described as "a genuine twentieth-century chamber music concert," included most of the songs the band were working on for their debut album release. Plus, they performed the A- and B-side of their next single: Originally called "Games for May," the disc was released as "See Emily Play" on June 16 and took Pink Floyd to No. 6 in the UK charts.

"See Emily Play" was recorded on May 21 with EMI producer Norman Smith in the production chair. In an attempt to reproduce the sound of "Arnold Layne," he decided to record the track at Sound Techniques, where the previous single had been created, rather than EMI's own studios at Abbey Road where the band had

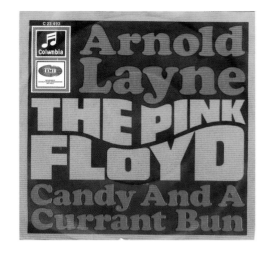

OPPOSITE: Outside London's UFO club, Tottenham Court Road, London, 1967

ABOVE: Vintage vinyl record, Pink Floyd, 1967

been recording other tracks since February. Like most of Pink Floyd's original material at that time, the single was conceived and written by Syd Barrett.

With its use of echo and reverb effects, and tapes slowed down or played backwards, the release was an early example of the "psychedelic" single which would become commonplace later in the year. Outside of the album market, only a couple of groups—including The Beatles—had made significant inroads into the singles arena with that kind of experimentation. Syd Barrett, however, was never happy with the release, being generally wary of singles as a sign of the band "selling out."

Notably, the others in the group were all too happy to indulge in the trappings of stardom that came with any chart success, especially three appearances on the BBC's flagship music show *Top of the Pops*. And it was on the third of those high-profile TV spots that Syd displayed quite publicly his disdain for the group's growing celebrity, with his erratic behavior which was becoming all too prevalent in their live performances generally.

Although he was the composer of the song—seemingly based on a real-life Emily, the offspring of a well-to-do Cambridge family who was known in UFO circles as the "psychedelic schoolgirl"—Syd had no inclination to promote it via the TV show. For the band's third appearance he merely sat on a cushion throughout their spot while the others lip-synced

## "If John Lennon doesn't have to do *Top of the Pops*, why should I?"

## Syd Barrett

to the track, apparently so stoned he was unable to stand up, let alone mime to his guitar part. He famously declared at the time: "If John Lennon doesn't have to do *Top of the Pops*, why should I?" Nevertheless, the single hit the charts a week after its release, climbing to No. 6, and remained in the best-sellers for the next three months—by which time Pink Floyd saw their debut album released, on August 4, 1967.

## The Album

Still acclaimed by die-hard Syd Barrett fans as Pink Floyd's greatest achievement, *The Piper at the Gates of Dawn* was an audacious first release by any standards. In many ways a clear indication of two aspects of the band at the time, the collection featured both the extended improvisations that dominated their live shows, and the less complex but equally challenging

songs composed by Barrett. Of eleven tracks, eight were written solely by Syd Barrett, while the two instrumentals were credited to all four members, and one song, "Take Up Thy Stethoscope and Walk"—a blistering evocation of two-chord transatlantic garage-punk—was written by Roger Waters.

Concurrent with a marked increase in his use of LSD through the three months of recording, Syd's numbers such as "The Gnome," "Matilda Mother," and "The Scarecrow" evoke the images (both light and dark) of childhood nursery rhymes and fairy stories. Likewise, the album's title was chosen by Barrett, from the 1908 children's book *The Wind in the Willows* by Kenneth Grahame.

But from the stark intro chords of the album opener, "Astronomy Dominé," there's also a nod to science fiction and other-worldly sound effects that were becoming the group's trademark sound, exemplified in the major instrumental on the album, the ten-minute "Interstellar Overdrive." It was all a long way from the down-the-line rhythm and blues that still characterized much of their repertoire just a year or so earlier. As one writer described the opening track: "With an intro so tense it might have been recorded on the brink of a black hole, Pink Floyd invent psychedelic space rock."

Alongside some dubious references in the UK tabloid press to Pink Floyd being a "drug" band, the album was generally well received in the music papers, with both the *New Musical Express* and *Record Mirror* awarding it four stars out of five. And it has stood the test of time: In 2007, referring specifically to Syd Barrett's contribution, the BBC Music website called it "a pinnacle of English psychedelic music . . . filled with the child-poet musings of a mind not yet

OPPOSITE: Pink Floyd, March 1967

ABOVE: L-R: Roger Waters, Nick Mason, Syd Barrett, and Rick Wright in the studio, 1967

oppressed, but free to wander between fairy tales and cosmic explorations and still be home in time for tea."

The album entered the UK chart on August 19, a fortnight after its release, and it remained there for fourteen more weeks, reaching the No. 6 position. Its success was perfectly in tune with the mood at the time: It reflected two key elements of "psychedelic" music—the flights of fancy evoking a child-like vision of the world, and the mind-boggling experimentation of musical sounds and techniques hitherto unheard of, especially in the world of commercial popular music.

There followed a complete repackaging of the album for the American market, where it was released simply as *Pink Floyd* on the Tower label, a subsidiary of Capitol Records, on October 21, 1967. "See Emily Play" was added to the track listing, while "Astronomy Dominé," "Flaming," and "Bike" did not appear at all. It failed to make any big impression on the US charts, peaking at No. 132.

Throughout the summer following the recording of the album, Syd became more and more unpredictable. The band were still playing regularly at UFO as well as on the wider UK rock circuit, but the guitarist's behavior was an increasing worry for the rest of the group and their management, with him sometimes being physically unable to take the stage. Even before the critical promotional appearances on *Top of the Pops*, Barrett's manner threatened to become a PR disaster for Pink Floyd—as when they were forced to cancel an appearance at the prestigious National Jazz and Blues Festival in August, on the weekend before the album release date. In a statement to the *New Musical Express*, co-manager Andrew King denied rumors that Syd had actually left the band: "It is not true that Syd has left the group. He is tired and exhausted, and has been advised to rest for two weeks."

It heralded the beginning of the end for Syd Barrett as a member of Pink Floyd, however. In December 1967 they brought in Syd's old friend the guitarist David Gilmour, initially to provide a fifth voice to the line-up, but at the end of January 1968 Syd Barrett's time in the group was brought to a final close. The next Pink Floyd album, which they began recording shortly after the release of *Piper*, would feature only one track written by Barrett—a far cry from his dominance as the key songwriter on their debut long-player.

OPPOSITE: Promotional shot of Pink Floyd, London, 1967

# The Piper at the Gates of Dawn

Track Listing (original UK vinyl release)
(All songs written by Syd Barrett except where indicated)

### Side One
Astronomy Dominé
Lucifer Sam
Matilda Mother
Flaming
Pow R. Toc H. (Syd Barrett, Roger Waters, Richard Wright, Nick Mason)
Take Up Thy Stethoscope and Walk (Waters)

### Side Two
Interstellar Overdrive (Barrett, Waters, Wright, Mason)
The Gnome
Chapter 24
The Scarecrow
Bike

| | |
|---|---|
| **Recorded:** | February 21 – May 21, 1967, EMI Studios, Abbey Road, London |
| **Released:** | August 4, 1967 (UK) |
| **Label:** | EMI Columbia |
| **Producer:** | Norman Smith |
| **Personnel:** | Syd Barrett (guitars, percussion, vocals), Roger Waters (bass guitar, whistle, percussion, vocals), Richard Wright (keyboards, cello, vibraphone, violin, percussion, vocals), Nick Mason (drums, percussion) |

**Chart Position:** UK No. 6

# a saucerful of secrets

"You have to remember Syd couldn't play guitar very well. David could. Syd had an attractive voice, but David had a great voice."

**Storm Thorgerson**

OPPOSITE: Pink Floyd, 1967

## Five Man Floyd

**S**yd Barrett's departure from Pink Floyd had been on the horizon since the cancelled dates of the previous summer. Following the Jazz and Blues Festival no-show, a vacation on the Spanish island of Formentera was set up under the auspices of Doctor Sam Hutt—a hip medical man familiar to many on the underground scene—to try to sort Syd out. The trip, however, which also involved Rick Wright and Roger Waters (not as patients it should be added!) with their respective girlfriends, was to no avail, with Barrett's state of mind continuing to get worse.

Despite their front man's decline, the band resumed working with some dates in Scandinavia, the Netherlands, and the UK, while sessions got under way for their next album. And in early November, after some delay involving work visas, Pink Floyd embarked on their first visit to the USA. *The Piper at the Gates of Dawn* (with an amended track listing) had been released in America on October 21, with a single from the album, "Flaming," hitting US record stores on November 6, though neither release made the American charts. The concert dates kicked off in San Francisco, at the Winterland Ballroom, on November 4, but from the start the short tour was fraught with problems.

OPPOSITE: Pink Floyd pictured with The Jimi Hendrix Experience, The Nice, Amen Corner, and The Move, 1967

ABOVE: 1967. L-R: Roger Waters, Nick Mason, Syd Barrett, Rick Wright.

For a start, venues like the 5,400-seater Winterland, and its sister concert space the Fillmore—where between the two arenas the band played four of its six US dates—were simply too big for the Floyd's limited array of equipment, and likewise their light show seemed sadly inadequate. And, of course, there was Syd, whose appetite for LSD and other drugs seemed more prodigious by the day. More often than not, his role onstage seemed limited to just standing there, stoned, or making contributions on the guitar that were totally irrelevant to the tune being played by the rest of the band. And things got even more critical when Pink Floyd made their debut appearances on US television.

On *The Pat Boone Show*, Dick Clark's *American Bandstand*, and the local Los Angeles program *Boss City*, Syd wouldn't answer interview questions with more than a single-word reply, and refused to lip-sync when the band were miming to various songs—songs that he himself had written! Following the embarrassment of these squandered promotional opportunities, Andrew King decided to draw a line under the whole affair by

cancelling some additional East Coast dates, and sending the band back to England.

There was some division among the management as to what to do next regarding Syd, with Peter Jenner more sympathetic to Barrett as the creative force behind much of what the band represented. "I never really got a coherent story of what happened in America. But I remember Andrew was shell shocked when he got back," Jenner would recall. "The trouble is I probably would have considered some of Syd's behaviour fine. It was avant-garde, and I thought avant-garde was cool."

Back in the UK, the band were booked onto a package tour headlined by The Jimi Hendrix Experience, and also featuring The Nice, Amen Corner, and The Move, plus two relative unknowns Eire Apparent and The Outer Limits. Although the exercise was good for the Floyd in as much as it gave them an insider view of the real world of rock touring for the first time—with all but the Hendrix group traveling in a communal tour bus—it turned into a nightmare where Syd's involvement was

concerned. The guitarist's performances became increasingly unreliable, to the point where he didn't show up at one date in Liverpool, and Dave O'List of The Nice took his place, with his back turned to the audience! O'List had watched Pink Floyd avidly during the previous tour nights and was confident enough to busk Barrett's parts fairly convincingly.

Overall, there was a growing feeling in the Floyd camp that Syd Barrett's days in the band were numbered, at least as a performing member of the line-up. While at one point Roger Waters demanded that Syd be fired on the spot, they settled on a proposal that he should be retained as an in-house songwriter, with his presence onstage augmented by an additional guitarist. With this five-piece formula in mind, in December 1967 the band approached Syd and Roger's old acquaintance from Cambridge David Gilmour.

David Jon Gilmour was born on March 6, 1946. His father, Douglas, was a lecturer in zoology at Cambridge University, and his mother, Sylvia, was a film editor at the BBC. He had his first taste of rock 'n' roll in the music's infancy, when he was barely in his teens, when he bought various records including Bill Haley's "Rock Around the Clock" and "Heartbreak Hotel" by Elvis Presley. And borrowing a guitar from a neighbor, he taught himself the fundamentals of the instrument, also nurturing a love of American blues along the way.

Gilmour first met up with Waters and Barrett when the latter were both at Cambridgeshire High School for Boys, just minutes away from the Perse School which he attended. In 1962, David enrolled at Cambridgeshire College of Arts and Technology to study modern languages, and he would spend his lunchtimes practicing guitar with Syd Barrett. Soon after he also joined his first group, a local blues-rock outfit called Jokers Wild. And he kept up his links with Barrett, to the extent that the two busked around France and Spain together during 1965.

A checkered musical period followed for Gilmour. In 1967, he teamed up in France with his ex-Jokers Wild colleagues Willie Wilson and Rick Wills to form Flowers (which later became Bullitt) but the trio failed to score on any level. Nevertheless, he did have a modicum of personal success in France when he recorded two lead vocals for the soundtrack of a film starring Brigitte Bardot, *Two Weeks in September*. But by the end of the year, David Gilmour was back in the UK, earning a non-musical living driving a van for the trendy fashion designer Ossie Clark. It was around this time that he became embroiled in the fortunes of Pink Floyd.

Gilmour had actually come across his old jamming partner Syd Barrett earlier in the year, when he attended one of the sessions for "See Emily Play," and was disturbed when Syd seemingly didn't recognize him. It was during a gig at the Royal College of Art on December 6 that Nick Mason recalls clapping eyes on Gilmour in the crowd, their paths having crossed on various occasions earlier. By that time Mason, Waters, and Wright had agreed that they should recruit a second guitarist to offset Syd's increasing unreliability, and Gilmour—at a loose end musically—seemed an ideal candidate. "As David was not a student I assumed he was there to check us out," Mason wrote in his 2004 memoir. "During a break I sidled up to David and muttered something about the possibility of him joining us as an additional guitarist. This was not a unilateral recruiting drive on my part, just the first chance any of us had had to broach the subject with him."

David Gilmour jumped at the chance to join the band, and between gigs throughout December they rehearsed the new five-piece line-up. In the words of Peter Jenner, the exercise was in order for Gilmour to "cover for Barrett's eccentricities," and to let Syd concentrate on contributing song material. Gilmour's place in the band, however, wasn't an entirely smooth transition: He would recall how "I actually walked out of one of the first rehearsals. Roger had got so unbearably awful, in a way that I'd later get used to, that I stomped out of the room." An omen of frictions further down the line?

## Floyd sans Syd

The first gigs with Gilmour were in the New Year, starting with a college appearance at Aston University, Birmingham, on January 12, 1968. Onstage, Syd was still a problem; while Gilmour covered for him on most of the guitar parts, Barrett's very presence—often silent and motionless—made for an awkward atmosphere between the two instrumentalists. The band also considered just keeping Syd on as songwriter, appearing onstage occasionally when he felt up to it. But Roger Waters was against that idea from the start, possibly because he saw himself as the future main composer in the group. The gigs involving both Syd Barrett and David Gilmour totaled just four, ending with an appearance on Hastings Pier on January 20, 1968.

Eventually, things came to a head regarding Syd, when the band decided not to pick him up for a date at Southampton University. It was January 26, and from there on the line-up onstage was just the four-piece. Barrett's actual departure from Pink Floyd wasn't officially decided until March, at a summit meeting involving the band—including Syd—and their management duo of Peter Jenner and Andrew King.

Jenner and King were staunch supporters of Barrett as the creative linchpin of Pink Floyd, and they decided then that they would represent Syd, rather than the four-piece without Syd. It was all agreed fairly amicably, and now they were no longer being managed by Blackhill Enterprises, the band looked to Bryan Morrison's agency for representation. Consequently, Morrison's booking agent Steve O'Rourke became Pink Floyd's manager, and remained so until his death in 2003.

On April 6, Syd Barrett's departure was announced officially, and a week later a single by the new line-up was released. After the chart success of "See Emily Play," the record company had been anxious to follow up with another hit in a similar vein, and in November 1967 had released "Apples and Oranges," recorded just three weeks earlier. But the Barrett-composed A-side, and its Rick Wright flip, "Paint Box," failed to emulate the triumph of "Emily," not appearing in the charts at all. So another single release, with the new formula Floyd regarding themselves primarily as an "album band," seemed something of a pointless exercise.

The single, which comprised a Rick Wright song, "It Would

> ## "I actually walked out of one of the first rehearsals. Roger had got so unbearably awful, in a way that I'd later get used to, that I stomped out of the room."
>
> ## David Gilmour

Be So Nice," and Roger Waters' "Julia Dream," confirmed the collective view that it was a commercially driven release that just didn't pay off. The faux-psychedelics of Wright's A-side contrasted badly with Syd Barrett's previous lyrical journeys in the same direction, and the record was another no-show chart-wise. Still coming to musical terms with Barrett's departure and Gilmour's arrival, none of the group were particularly enthusiastic about the release. As Nick Mason would reflect: "At that period we had no direction. We were being hustled about to make hit singles. There's so many people saying it's important you start to think it is important. It is possible on an LP to do exactly what we want to do."

## The Album

The band had been accumulating tracks for a second album since the middle of 1967, soon after the release of their debut long-player. So there was already a body of material featuring Syd Barrett, added to which tracks were laid down with his replacement, David Gilmour, when they reconvened in early 1968 at EMI's Abbey Road studios. In the event, only one song on the album would be a Syd Barrett composition, and the former front man would feature on just two other tracks as guitarist.

The first track recorded for the album, on August 8, 1967, was Roger Waters' "Set the Controls for the Heart of the Sun." It would be the only track to feature all five Pink Floyd members, after David Gilmour overdubbed some guitar parts in January and February—although the guitars from both musicians became buried somewhat in the final mix. One of Waters' earliest compositions, the song is a marker of where the bass player took over from Barrett as the band's prime songwriter. Set in the hippie heartland of sci-fi music effects and flying saucers, some of the lyrics were revealed by Waters to have actually originated in ancient Chang Dynasty Chinese poetry. The outer space epic would become one of the band's most popular anthems with concert audiences.

Two other songs written solely by Roger Waters were the opener, "Let There Be More Light," and the virulently anti-war "Corporal Clegg." The former song was certainly a pointer to the bass player's rapidly maturing songwriting, with its references to literary sci-fi heroes. The latter, a rare slice of social comment at this stage in Pink Floyd's recording career, was an aggressive outburst of musical anger, at odds with the air of detachment pervading most of the album.

Aside from "Set the Controls for the Heart of the Sun," the only other tracks involving Syd Barrett were Richard Wright's "Remember a Day," on which the keyboard man provided the vocals, and Syd's composition "Jugband Blues." Rick's song was another excursion into the somewhat twee territory of childhood nostalgia, more often associated with Barrett's acid-inspired lyrics. Wright would

continue in that same vein with the album's penultimate track, "See-Saw." Barrett's full involvement as vocalist and composer comes in the album's final track, on which he enlisted the help of a Salvation Army brass band to add some bizarre effects—first evoking a jolly street parade, but soon descending into sonic chaos. It's a bitter-sweet finale to the album, made all the more poignant in the context of Syd Barrett's departure from Pink Floyd.

The title track of the collection, which opened Side Two on the original vinyl release, was a classic Pink Floyd set-piece. A basically instrumental opus (with some wordless vocal effects from Gilmour and Wright), the nearly twelve-minute work was divided into four parts: "Something Else," "Syncopated Pandemonium," "Storm Signal," and "Celestial Voices." With neither able to read music, Roger Waters and Nick Mason—both former architecture students—devised a system of notation that more than one observer described as akin to architectural diagrams. The shifting musical atmosphere in each section highlighted the band's skill in using contrasting sonic dynamics—up-tempo and slow, loud and quiet—to stimulate emotional reactions in the listener. Plus of course, they employed the highly effective tacit punctuation of the sound of silence. Influences on the music clearly included Rick Wright's predilection for the free-form jazz of John Coltrane and Archie Shepp, and Roger Waters' interest in avant-garde classical music by the likes of John Cage.

An outstanding feature of the album was its cover. After The Beatles it was only the second time that EMI Records had allowed an act to choose an outside

OPPOSITE: Guitarist and lead singer David Gilmour, circa 1970

ABOVE: Pink Floyd at London's BBC Studios, circa 1967

designer as opposed to an in-house team, and Pink Floyd turned to their old friend Storm Thorgerson, who Roger Waters, Syd Barrett, and David Gilmour all knew from the Cambridge scene. Thorgerson had attended Cambridgeshire High School for Boys alongside Syd and Roger, and had also known David Gilmour as a teenager.

With fellow designer Aubrey "Po" Powell, Thorgerson set up the Hipgnosis company in 1968, and *A Saucerful of Secrets* was their first venture into album cover design. With thirteen separate images superimposed on one another, it was one of the first truly psychedelic sleeves to appear in the UK. Relegating any hint of a picture of the band to one small image, the montage consisted of what Powell referred to as "cosmic swirls," flying saucers, moons, and planets, and an appearance by Marvel Comics' Doctor Strange.

The album was released on June 28, 1968, and received mainly favorable reviews. Despite the *New Musical Express* calling it "long and boring," the influential DJ John Peel went as far as describing a live performance of the title track as "like a religious experience." And even a muted review in the *Melody Maker*—"their experiments in jazz, pop, contemporary serious music and electronics indicate a merger of thought rather than a divergence"—concluded with the advice to readers: "Give the Floyd a listen—it isn't really so painful." And many fans clearly did just that, with the album reaching the No. 9 position in the UK charts.

As an interested party regarding the fortunes of the group, Storm Thorgerson recognized the significance of Syd Barrett's departure and David Gilmour's entry into the line-up: "You have to remember Syd couldn't play guitar very well. David could. Syd had an attractive voice, but David had a great voice." And in retrospect, Nick Mason for one would cite the album as his favorite by Pink Floyd, as the only tangible link between the essential eras of the band marked by the presence of both Barrett and his successor, Gilmour: "I think [it] was a quite good way of marking Syd's departure and Dave's arrival," he said to *Newsweek* magazine in 2014. "It's rather nice to have it on one record, where you get both things. It's a cross-fade rather than a cut."

OPPOSITE: A new line-up. L-R: Nick Mason, Dave Gilmour, Rick Wright (center front), Roger Waters, August 1968, Los Angeles

# A Saucerful of Secrets

Track Listing (original UK vinyl release)

### Side One
Let There Be More Light (Roger Waters)
Remember a Day (Richard Wright)
Set the Controls for the Heart of the Sun (Waters)
Corporal Clegg (Waters)

### Side Two
A Saucerful of Secrets (Waters, Wright, Nick Mason, David Gilmour)
See-Saw (Wright)
Jugband Blues (Syd Barrett)

| | |
|---|---|
| **Recorded:** | August 1967 – May 1968, EMI Studios, Abbey Road, London; De Lane Lea Studios, London |
| **Released:** | June 28, 1968 (UK), July 27, 1968 (US) |
| **Label:** | EMI Columbia (UK), Tower (US) |
| **Producer:** | Norman Smith |
| **Personnel:** | David Gilmour (guitars, kazoo, vocals), Roger Waters (bass guitar, percussion, vocals), Richard Wright (Farfisa organ, Hammond organ, Mellotron, vibraphone, celeste, xylophone, tin whistle, vocals), Nick Mason (drums, percussion, kazoo, vocals), Syd Barrett (slide guitar, acoustic guitar, electric guitar, vocals) |

**Additional Personnel:**
Norman Smith (drums, vocals), Stanley Myers Orchestra, Salvation Army International Staff Band

**Chart Position:** UK No. 9

# more

"It's hard to say what I thought of our music in *More* since I didn't see it with the film, but apparently it works quite well. As an album I don't really much like it."

**Rick Wright**

OPPOSITE: Roy Harper at the Cambridge Folk Festival, 1968

ABOVE: Pink Floyd in Zurich, Switzerland, 1968

## On the Road

The day after the release of *A Saucerful of Secrets*, on June 29, 1968, Pink Floyd topped the bill at the first ever free rock concert to be held in London's Hyde Park. Also appearing at the "Midsummer High Weekend" show were singer-songwriter Roy Harper (who joined Pink Floyd onstage to play cymbals on "A Saucerful of Secrets"), Jethro Tull, and a new acoustic duo fronted by Marc Bolan, Tyrannosaurus Rex; the event was staged by the Floyd's ex-management company, Blackhill Enterprises. For Pink Floyd the concert was a huge success, where they were able to perform songs from their new album in front of a crowd of over fifteen thousand. It was in a subsequent review of the gig that John Peel would rhapsodize about their rendition of the title track as "like a religious experience," in the next edition of *Disc* magazine.

Immediately following the success of the Hyde Park concert, just over a week later the band were playing at the Kinetic Playground in Chicago, on the first night of their second American tour. This trip seemed better coordinated than the last abortive visit to the US, and without the distractions of Syd Barrett's erratic behavior. For most of the dates they shared the bill with various other UK bands

who were already big names in the US, including The Who, The Troggs, and Herman's Hermits—plus their old comrades from UFO, Soft Machine.

There was still an element of unpreparedness regarding the tour, including a quick trip to Canada in order to obtain work visas, the band having arrived holding only tourist permits. And again in most cases their stage equipment seemed inadequate for the venues, not least at the 100,000-seater JFK Stadium, where they played at the Philadelphia Music Festival (billed as "The English Invasion," with advance tickets at one dollar) alongside The Who and The Troggs. The large venues contrasted with the Scene club in New York, where they played a short three-night residency to a more dedicated audience of bona fide Pink Floyd enthusiasts.

Whatever the shortcomings of this second transatlantic visit, it helped raise the US profile of the band, and in doing so helped in the promotion of *A Saucerful of Secrets*, which had been

released on July 27, right in the middle of the tour. The album, however, would make no impression on the American charts.

A week after their return from the States, the band were on the road again, kicking off a full diary of dates in the UK and Europe at the Kastival 68 festival in Kasterlee, Belgium, at the end of August. There followed solid gigging through to the end of the year, with dates in Switzerland, Germany, and France, as well as the now well-worn circuit of venues across the United Kingdom.

The latter included an appearance at Middle Earth, the venue at the Roundhouse in London's Chalk Farm which had taken over as the center of the capital's "psychedelic scene" after the demise of UFO the previous year. Calling Middle Earth "that last London bastion of hippiedom and the Underground generally," journalist Hugh Nolan described how "your true underground music freak thinks nothing of staying at London's Roundhouse until the grim grey reality of six o'clock in the morning."

But now Pink Floyd's ambitions went beyond the parameters of the so-called Underground; with two albums under their belt—both of which had made it to the Top Ten of the UK albums chart—they were keen to consolidate the kind of mass recognition that had eluded them with Syd Barrett as their creative driving force. And with bands like The Yardbirds, Cream, Jimi Hendrix, and The Who now having albums scoring as strongly as singles, in the words of Joe Boyd, "The Underground was becoming the mainstream."

The almost continuous touring across the UK and mainland Europe continued into 1969, but not before the band had another stab (presumably in response to pressure from EMI Records) at the singles chart. Recorded on November 4, 1968, and released a month later, "Point Me at the Sky" was an early writing collaboration between Roger Waters and Dave Gilmour, but like the band's previous two singles the record failed to make any impact on the charts. However, the instrumental B-side, "Careful with That Axe, Eugene," credited to Waters, Wright, Mason, and Gilmour, proved to be popular, featuring in their stage set for some time to come, and appearing on various live and compilation albums over the years.

## On the Screen

The gigs on the road included two live recording sessions that would appear on Pink Floyd's album *Ummagumma*, released in November 1969. They were at Mothers club in Birmingham, and Manchester College of Commerce, on April 27 and May 2 respectively. But prior to that, the band were in the studio

RIGHT: A group portrait while touring Europe, Zurich, Switzerland, 1968

ABOVE: Vintage record sleeve for Pink Floyd's "Point Me at the Sky," 1968

A FILM BY PETER WHITEHEAD

# TONITE LETS ALL MAKE
# LOVE IN LONDON.

ALAN ALDRIDGE     EDNA O'BRIEN     PINK FLOYD
DAVID HOCKNEY     ANDREW OLDHAM     MICHAEL CAINE
SMALL FACES     VASHTI     TWICE AS MUCH
LEE MARVIN     MICK JAGGER     GENEVIEVE
ALAN GINSBERG     JULIE CHRISTIE     CHRIS FARLOWE
MARQUESS OF KENSINGTON

through January and February, laying down the music for the soundtrack to the film *More*, which would also constitute their third studio album, to be released in June.

It wasn't the first time Pink Floyd had been involved in filmmaking of one kind or another. In 1967 they had appeared in the now-legendary documentary directed by Peter Whitehead *Tonite Let's All Make Love in London*, which focused on the nascent psychedelic scene in the capital. As well as now-historic interviews with the likes of John Lennon, Allen Ginsberg, Mick Jagger, Michael Caine, Julie Christie, and many other celebrities of the era, footage included sequences at the "14 Hour Technicolor Dream" event in April '67, and scenes shot at UFO, both featuring the band. During the seventy-two-minute film Pink Floyd perform "Interstellar Overdrive" no less than four times, in various truncated takes. A 1990 rerelease of the soundtrack music and interviews included the closest on record to their sixteen-minute Syd Barrett-era stage version of the number.

Then in December 1967, the Floyd were commissioned to provide the music for a *Tomorrow's World* documentary on BBC Television, featuring the

OPPOSITE: Roger Waters performing with Pink Floyd at Bristol University, UK, March 3, 1969

ABOVE: A promotional poster for *Tonite Let's All Make Love in London*, a documentary about the city's nascent psychedelic scene

heard by the characters at the time. So it might be a snippet from a song on the radio, a tune on a café jukebox, the ambient noise at a party. As Roger Waters would explain it, "He wanted the soundtrack to relate exactly to what was happening in the movie, rather than a film score backing the visuals."

On its release in August 1969, the film itself met with muted reviews, and it was certainly not the success among the movie-going cognoscenti (of France in particular) that an aspiring "art-house" director like Schroeder might have hoped for. But it was popular with general cinema audiences around Europe, its profile raised by the release of the Pink Floyd soundtrack album two months earlier.

## The Album

While EMI Records didn't have a problem with Pink Floyd working on a film soundtrack per se, as it was a private commission outside their contract with the company, the band were not allowed to utilize Abbey Road Studios or their previous producer Norman Smith. Instead they used Pye Studios, near London's Marble Arch, producing the recording themselves with the aid of in-house engineer Brian Humphries, with Norman Smith simply credited as "executive producer."

To fulfill Barbet Schroeder's brief of creating "mood" pieces to accompany specific sequences, the band watched the film in a viewing theater, timing each section on a stopwatch. They then went into the studio, creating the soundtrack piece-by-piece: Engineer Humphries was amazed when the whole process was completed in just a couple of weeks. Most of the songs as such were written by Roger Waters, while the more collaborative instrumental pieces on the album were full of what Nick Mason described as the "rumblings, squeaks, and sound textures" that were now one of the trademarks of their live shows.

experimental light shows of their one-time landlord Mike Leonard. And in 1968 the band provided soundtrack music for a British film noir thriller *The Committee*, starring R&B vocalist Paul Jones in an acting role as the lead character. Years later Nick Mason opined that their contribution to the soundtrack had been more a series of sound effects than actual music.

Written and directed by Barbet Schroeder—a protégé of the great Jean-Luc Godard, and an up-and-coming name among the French avant-garde—*More* was in many ways a cautionary swansong to the excesses of the "Swinging Sixties." The storyline concerned a young German student who hitch-hikes to Paris, gets embroiled with a hedonistic crowd and an American heroin-addicted girl in particular, and commences a downward spiral of drug abuse on the island of Ibiza—where he ends his own life in a suicidal overdose.

The film was virtually finished when Schroeder offered Pink Floyd the commission to provide the music, and early in 1969 they laid down the music for what was not a soundtrack in the traditional sense. Where film scores are usually for "background" music that enhances the plot, often drives the action, and captures the audience's attention, Schroeder wanted "source" music consisting of what was being

Nearer to what could be called a conventional song than many tracks on the album, the opener, "Cirrus Minor," is Roger Waters in archetypal spaced-out mode. The speedy efficiency of the band's sonic creativity that impressed Brian Humphries was matched by Waters' productivity where the words were concerned, writing most of the lyrics for the songs between breaks in laying down the backing tracks. David Gilmour's double-tracked vocals were backed with an organ-

OPPOSITE: Poster for British film *The Committee*, 1968

RIGHT: Vinyl record sleeve for *Live in Amsterdam Fantasio Club*, recorded in 1968 and released in 1987

# more

when two people love, one always loves more

dominant delivery, with percussionist Mason absent altogether.

Two of the tracks, "The Nile Song" and "Ibiza Bar," were released as a single—without success—in Japan, New Zealand, and France. The reasoning behind the coupling may have been that both songs featured Gilmour in more of a straight-ahead rock mold than was usual with Pink Floyd, and Nick Mason too sounds more in sync with the heavy blues percussion of contemporary bands like Cream and The Jimi Hendrix Experience. The slow instrumental "More Blues" was also in similar style, and went on to be a regular feature as the encore in the band's stage sets.

Other songs which in the movie appeared as mere snippets were lengthened considerably in live performance, including Roger Waters' three-minute "Green Is the Colour," a folky but evocative love song delivered by Dave Gilmour (who handled all the lead vocals on the album), with some enhancing tin whistle played by Nick's then-wife Lindy Mason. And Lindy also appeared on the "Party Sequence," which closed the first side of the vinyl release. A percussion-based evocation of hippie good times, the one-minute blast featured the Mason couple on congas and tin whistle, with the rest of the band helping out rhythmically; it was one of six tracks in total credited to all four members.

An excursion into nightmare territory (indeed, in later live performances the song was renamed "Nightmare"), "Cymbaline" reflects the potential horror involved in a bad drug trip, referencing the Marvel Comics character Doctor Strange in the process. The band went on to play "Cymbaline" in concert from early 1969 until their final show of 1971, making it the longest-lasting number from *More* to be featured live onstage.

Reviews at the time in both the music and mainstream press were mixed, as would be expected for what was basically a movie soundtrack album. The film was premiered at the Cannes Film Festival in May 1969, but made negligible impact, so it came as something of a surprise to many when the album actually crept into the UK Top Ten at No. 9. And the band themselves weren't clear as to their overall view of the exercise. On reflection a few months later, Rick Wright admitted: "It's hard to say what I thought of our music in *More* since I didn't see it with the film, but apparently it works quite well. As an album I don't really much like it."

OPPOSITE: A poster for Barbet Schroeder's 1969 drama *More* starring Mimsy Farmer and Klaus Grünberg

# More

Track Listing (original UK vinyl release)

### Side One
Cirrus Minor (Roger Waters)
The Nile Song (Waters)
Crying Song (Waters)
Up the Khyber (Nick Mason, Richard Wright)
Green Is the Colour (Waters)
Cymbaline (Waters)
Party Sequence (Waters, Wright, Mason, David
    Gilmour)

### Side Two
Main Theme (Waters, Wright, Mason, Gilmour)
Ibiza Bar (Waters, Wright, Mason, Gilmour)
More Blues (Waters, Wright, Mason, Gilmour)
Quicksilver (Waters, Wright, Mason, Gilmour)
A Spanish Piece (Gilmour)
Dramatic Theme (Waters, Wright, Mason, Gilmour)

| | |
|---|---|
| **Recorded:** | January–February, 1969, Pye Studios, London |
| **Released:** | June 13, 1969 (UK), August 9, 1969 (US) |
| **Label:** | EMI Columbia (UK), Tower (US) |
| **Producer:** | Pink Floyd |
| **Personnel:** | David Gilmour (guitars, percussion, vocals), Roger Waters (bass guitar, percussion, vocals), Richard Wright (Farfisa organ, Hammond organ, vibraphone, vocals), Nick Mason (drums, percussion, bongos) |

**Additional Personnel:**
    Lindy Mason (tin whistle)

**Chart Position:** UK No. 9

# ummagumma

**"I don't think we were that taken with it. It was fun to make, however, and a useful exercise, the individual sections proving, to my mind, that the parts were not as great as the sum."**

**Nick Mason**

OPPOSITE: Pink Floyd, circa 1970

## Gigging

**B**etween the recording and release of the *More* soundtrack, Pink Floyd were touring the UK virtually continuously. Apart from two French dates—a TV show in Paris and a festival in Bordeaux—all of nearly sixty gigs through to the end of June 1969 were scattered across the length and breadth of England, Scotland, and Wales.

Among the obligatory bookings at places like the Dome, Brighton, the Van Dike Club in Plymouth, and an abundance of college venues, there were the more left-field engagements—benefits and such—linked to the Floyd's continuing association with the counterculture. The latter included an Edinburgh benefit concert for the homeless charity Shelter, a fundraiser for Glasgow Arts Lab, and a spot at the Camden Free Festival in London. Plus there were two dates that stood out from the mainly run-of-the-mill bookings on the UK rock circuit, both of the band's own devising.

The first show, which came at the close of the spring tour, was staged at London's Royal Festival Hall on April 14. With the audacious title "The Massed Gadgets of Auximenes – More Furious Madness from Pink Floyd," the concert involved the reintroduction of the Azimuth Co-ordinator, the massive surround-sound apparatus that had graced the band's Games for May concert at the Queen Elizabeth Hall back in May 1967.

The "happening" (for that was what it truly was) involved taped sound effects as well as live music, performance art as the band built a table on the stage then

OPPOSITE: Syd Barrett, 1969, around the time of recording his debut solo album *The Madcap Laughs*

ABOVE: Roger Waters appears in a back projection for Pink Floyd's show Games for May, Queen Elizabeth Hall, London, May 12, 1967

drank tea while a radio was tuned in randomly, and a gas-masked "monster" roaming the audience—the latter an old friend of the band from their Stanhope Gardens days. The entire conceptual event was split into two parts, "The Man" and "The Journey," the musical content of which was drawn from songs the band had recorded or were about to, and formed the basis for their next sequence of tour dates in the UK.

A review by *Melody Maker* journalist Chris Welch captured some of the ambience of the occasion, describing how "burbling bird calls twittered overhead depicting daybreak, a mood broken by the group hammering and sawing up amplified logs, symbolizing the day's work, followed by sleep, nightmares and

ABOVE: Roger Waters photographed with his first wife, Judy Trim

> # "A friend of mine . . . was very disappointed and felt cheated. He thought it was like paying fifteen bob to see us rehearsing. He was right in a way because we were rehearsing. The people were watching a happening."
>
> ## Roger Waters

a return to daybreak," concluding "A stream of events held our attention. In parts the pace flagged and it seemed the machines were in danger of playing the group. As straight players, they have enough technique and more enthusiasm."

Interviewed by Welch a couple of weeks later, Roger Waters was circumspect in his appraisal of the concert: "It was a nerve racking experience for us, and probably the audience. A friend of mine who comes to see our normal stage act was very disappointed and felt cheated. He thought it was like paying fifteen bob to see us rehearsing. He was right in a way because we were rehearsing. The people were watching a happening."

Rehearsal or not, the music (although not most of the special effects) formed the basis for the UK "The Man / Journey" tour that followed. In most venues the songs were presented alongside the band's usual material, until the Royal Albert Hall date on June 26 when, as one writer put it, "Waters' desire for a spectacle peaked with 'The Final Lunacy.'" The already ambitious scenario presented at the Festival Hall was now embellished with a section of the Royal Philharmonic Orchestra and the Ealing Central Amateur Choir, Richard Wright tackling the Albert Hall's vast church-style organ, and the firing of two cannons which were usually employed in performances of the *1812 Overture*.

Prior to the Albert Hall date, Dave Gilmour and Roger Waters were also involved in studio work with Syd Barrett, on what would be Syd's first solo album, *The Madcap Laughs*. The former Floyd lead man had already recorded parts of the album when he called upon his ex-colleagues to help out, mainly on the production side. The sessions hardly went smoothly, however, with various tracks being abandoned half-finished, to be completed at a further date in July. In all, the two Pink Floyd musicians were involved in seven of the thirteen tracks on the album, which was eventually released in January 1970.

## Recording

Two other dates from Pink Floyd's early-year tour were of significance, in that they were the venues for the live recordings that formed the first part of their next album, *Ummagumma*, which would appear in November 1969. The first recordings took place at a gig at Mothers club in Birmingham on April 27, and the second five days later at the Manchester College of Commerce. Described by Nick Mason as "a kind of Midlands version of Middle Earth," Mothers in the Erdington district of Birmingham was a favorite among most of the bands touring the UK rock club circuit in the late 1960s. Between 1968 and the New Year of 1971, it played host to a plethora of rock royalty that included Fleetwood Mac, The Who, Elton John, and Led Zeppelin, plus a variety of American visitors ranging from Canned Heat and The Grateful Dead to the blues legends Muddy Waters and Son House.

The idea of the live tracks was to present onstage versions of numbers that the fans were already familiar with, before the band subsequently dropped them from their repertoire, as Roger Waters explained to *Melody Maker*: "The four songs on the first album are a set of numbers that we'd been playing all round the country for a long time, and we decided to record them before we jacked them in. And they've changed a lot since we first recorded them."

The band recorded an additional appearance the night prior to the Mothers set, at Bromley Technical College, but it was not used for the album. Of the live recordings used—"Astronomy Dominé," "Careful with That Axe, Eugene," "Set the Controls for the Heart of the Sun," and "A Saucerful of Secrets"—only the last number, according to Richard Wright, was a composite of both sessions: "The live part of the album we had to record twice. The first time, at Mothers in Birmingham, we felt we'd played really well, but the equipment didn't work so we couldn't

OPPOSITE: Storm Thorgerson (1944-2013), graphic designer and video director, pictured in 1967

LEFT: Musician and record producer Norman Smith (1923-2008), also known as Hurricane Smith, circa 1971

use nearly all of that one. The second time, at Manchester College of Commerce, was a really bad gig but as the recording equipment was working well, we had to use it . . . parts of 'Saucer' on *Ummagumma* came from the Birmingham gig which we put together with the Manchester stuff."

The resultant four-track live album encapsulated for all time Pink Floyd as they sounded onstage in 1969. Syd Barrett's "Astronomy Dominé" garnered all the rock band power, amply extended to over eight-and-a-half minutes, that the Floyd were capable of. Likewise, "Careful with That Axe . . ." and "Set the Controls . . ." were both given the additional instrumental attention each deserved, while nearly thirteen minutes of "Saucerful . . ." was in fact a modest treatment compared to the twenty-odd served up to audiences on many occasions.

In between dates through the late summer and autumn of 1969, which as well as the well-worn UK rock circuit included gigs in Belgium, the Netherlands, and Germany, the band managed to fit in enough studio time to complete the second disc of their upcoming double album. On the suggestion of in-house producer Norman Smith, each member of the group brought their own home-created demos into Abbey Road to be prepared for inclusion. The idea was originally sparked by Rick Wright, who wanted an LP divided into four solo contributions, each without the involvement of the others.

Wright's classically influenced section, "Sysyphus," opened the first side. Named after the character in Greek mythology, more commonly spelled as Sisyphus (who was condemned

forever to push a boulder up a hill, only for it to roll back down when he reached the top), the four-part concert piece had Wright on various keyboards, with the only addition being that of Norman Smith on percussion. The sheer dynamic of the track, culminating in what many heard as a chaos of cacophony, was certainly startling—though many, including Wright not long afterwards, would condemn the track as simply pretentious.

There followed two compositions by Roger Waters, "Grantchester Meadows," and the indulgently titled "Several Species of Small Furry Animals Gathered Together in a Cave and Grooving with a Pict." "Grantchester" was classic Floyd lyricism, an idyllic English countryside evoked via background birdsong and a simple acoustic guitar, the sound of absent Syd still present in elements of Roger's coy delivery. The second Waters contribution involved no conventional instrumentation, just a collection of tape and electronic effects conjoined rhythmically by the repetition of recorded snippets of the singer's voice, sounding like beatbox ahead of its time.

David Gilmour's "The Narrow Way" was another piece divided into sections, its three parts forming a twelve-minute panoply of guitar dynamics. With overdubbed acoustic guitars giving way to echo-laden special effects, the piece concludes with some ethereal vocals penned and delivered by the guitarist— seemingly Gilmour had asked Waters to provide some words for the exercise, only to be turned down by the bass player.

The track from Nick Mason thankfully avoided an exhibitionist drum solo, that mainstay of many a rock band's performance in the late sixties. Instead the percussionist treated listeners to fairly laid-back meanderings around the drum kit evoking the exotic atmosphere of "The Grand Vizier's Garden Party." In fact Mason's "solo" effort owed more to some of the sonic ramblings of free-form Euro-jazz than mainstream rock. The three-parter was also bookended by flute contributions from Nick's wife Lindy, who was an accomplished instrumentalist in her own right.

Nick had married Lindy Rutter in 1968, having known her since his days as a teenager at Frensham Heights co-educational school. Roger Waters also married a childhood sweetheart, Judith Trim, a potter and school teacher. The couple wed in 1969, and Judith appeared on the gatefold sleeve of *Ummagumma* when it was originally released. And Richard Wright had married Juliette Gale in 1964, Juliette having sung with formative Floyd line-ups, including Sigma 6, as early as 1963. In an industry characterized by fragile relationships, the Pink Floyd of 1969 seemed a model of marital stability, with David Gilmour (who wouldn't marry until 1975) the only singleton in the line-up.

## Release

When the double album was released in November 1969, the immediate point of conversation was the front cover image. Designed by Storm Thorgerson's Hipgnosis team, who had created the cover art for both *A Saucerful of Secrets* and the *More* soundtrack album, it avoided the "psychedelic" treatment applied to both those releases. Instead, it ushered in a phase of using hyperreal photographic images that were as unsettling as the visual distortion of the previous artworks. In the case of *Ummagumma*, a picture of the band includes the exact same picture hanging on a wall, achieving what in design terms is called a Droste effect, where the image is then repeated ad infinitum—or, in reality, duplicated as far as the photographic resolution and scale of the picture allow it.

It was before the days of computer-aided imagery of any kind, and it marked Hipgnosis's graphic style—and the imagery associated with Pink Floyd over no less than ten albums—for some years to come. As Thorgerson would explain: "If we arranged some kind of . . . set or some kind of grouping of people or some kind of event, or some kind of sculpture or installation, we would set it up and shoot it. We might shoot it in bits, but it would all be shot for real. And that, I think, is because in some ineffable fashion, it's always better. It's always better. Obviously you can do all sorts of things in a computer that look better for doing them in a computer, but they are computer things."

The release was also marked by it being on EMI's new label aimed at the "progressive" rock market, Harvest, launched in June 1969. It was another sign that what was considered "underground" just a year or so before, and outside the usual

remit of an established record company like EMI, was now being treated as part of the commercial mainstream. As the head of the new label, Malcolm Jones, explained to *Melody Maker*: "EMI, as a major record company, had no policy against underground groups when I joined the company. But the smaller independent companies tended to grab the sort of artists and groups I am now signing for Harvest." And, already being signed to EMI, Pink Floyd were at the forefront of this change in focus on the part of the music business establishment.

For an album that could fairly be described as patchy in many respects, *Ummagumma* did surprisingly well in terms of actual over-the-counter sales—especially for a more costly double album. As well as reaching the No. 5 spot in the UK album charts at the time, over the years it went on to earn Gold disc certification in France and Germany, plus a Platinum rating in the USA when it eventually cleared over a million. And critical reception was generally positive, with several magazines—including *Vox* and the *International Times*—particularly enthusiastic about the live half of the release. In retrospect, the band themselves were less than glowing in their assessment of the project, with Dave Gilmour calling it "horrible," Nick Mason admitting the band were not "that taken with it" from the start, and Roger Waters declaring, "What a disaster!"

# Ummagumma

Track Listing (original UK vinyl release)

### Side One
Astronomy Dominé (Syd Barrett)
Careful with That Axe, Eugene (Roger Waters,
    Richard Wright, Nick Mason, David Gilmour)

### Side Two
Set the Controls for the Heart of the Sun (Waters)
A Saucerful of Secrets (Waters, Wright, Mason,
    Gilmour)
    I. Something Else
    II. Syncopated Pandemonium
    III. Storm Signal
    IV. Celestial Voices

### Side Three
Sysyphus (Wright)
    Part I
    Part II
    Part III
    Part IV
Grantchester Meadows (Waters)
Several Species of Small Furry Animals Gathered
    Together in a Cave and Grooving with a Pict
    (Waters)

### Side Four
The Narrow Way (Gilmour)
    Part I
    Part II
    Part III
The Grand Vizier's Garden Party (Mason)
    Part I: Entrance
    Part II: Entertainment
    Part III: Exit

**Recorded:** Live album: April 27, 1969, Mothers, Birmingham; May 2, 1969, Manchester College of Commerce. Studio album: various dates, EMI Studios, Abbey Road, London

**Released:** November 7, 1969 (UK), November 8, 1969 (US)

**Label:** Harvest

**Producer:** Pink Floyd, Norman Smith

**Personnel:** David Gilmour (guitars, drums, percussion, keyboards, vocals), Roger Waters (bass guitar, guitars, vocals), Richard Wright (organ, Mellotron, vibraphone, percussion, vocals), Nick Mason (drums, percussion)

**Additional Personnel:** Lindy Mason (flutes)

**Chart Position:** UK No. 5, US No. 74, Netherlands No. 5

OPPOSITE: Pink Floyd, circa 1970

# atom heart mother

"I listened to that album recently: God, it's shit, possibly our lowest point artistically. It sounds like we didn't have any idea between us."

### David Gilmour

OPPOSITE: David Gilmour performing with Pink Floyd at the Hyde Park Free Concert, London, July 18, 1970

## Zabriskie Point

**A**lmost immediately after the release of *Ummagumma*, Pink Floyd deviated from the usual routine of following an album with a promotional tour, by instead embarking on another film soundtrack project. The eminent Italian director Michelangelo Antonioni—best known for his early-sixties trilogy of *L'Avventura*, *La Notte*, and *L'Eclisse*, and the English-language cult classic from 1966 *Blow-Up*—had first seen the band playing at the *International Times* launch party at London's Roundhouse in 1966. Familiar with their soundtrack work on *The Committee* and more recently the French avant-garde film *More*, Antonioni felt that Pink Floyd would be perfect to create the music for his next film, *Zabriskie Point*.

Homing in on the countercultural landscape much as *Blow-Up* had done successfully three years earlier, the film followed an American student who flees a violent campus confrontation with the police, steals a plane, and ends up in Death Valley, California. With a hippie girlfriend in the mix, the plot offered a potent scenario of radical politics, psychedelic flower-power, graphic sex, and social breakdown that seemed a perfect combination for the times.

In November 1969, Antonioni booked the band into the luxurious Hotel Massimo d'Azeglio in Rome, where they would be based for two weeks while they

Movie still (above) and promotional poster (opposite) for the cult Michelangelo Antonioni film *Zabriskie Point*, 1970

> **"Antonioni's not hard to work with . . . but he's a perfectionist . . . It was hard, but it was worth it."**
>
> **Rick Wright**

A FILM BY MICHELANGELO ANTONIONI

ZABRISKIE POINT

AN MGM PRESENTATION

worked on the soundtrack at a nearby studio. On account of the studio being booked at short notice, the only time available was between midnight and nine in the morning, so for the rest of the time the band either slept, or valiantly tried to use up the generous per-day allowance for food and drink provided by the film company, MGM.

Unfortunately, the soundtrack didn't progress as anticipated, with the director never quite satisfied with the "finished" tapes the band had produced over the previous night. As Nick Mason would recall: "Each piece had to be finished rather than roughed out, then redone, rejected, and resubmitted." Rick Wright, however, had a more positive view of the sessions, in an interview given at the time: "It's all improvised, but nonetheless it was really hard work. We had each piece of music and we did about, say, six takes of each, and he'd choose the best. Antonioni's not hard to work with . . . but he's a perfectionist . . . It was hard, but it was worth it."

But in the event, when the movie was released in February 1970, the soundtrack included just three tracks by Pink Floyd, alongside contributions from The Grateful Dead, John Fahey, and others. The Floyd numbers were the instrumental "Heart Beat, Pig Meat," the uncharacteristic country-flavored "Crumbling Land," and "Come In Number 51, Your Time Is Up," a reworking of "Careful with That Axe, Eugene" from 1968.

Nevertheless, the soundtrack album, released in the March, was more favorably received than the actual film, the latter bombing at the box office.

And the band, following an already established policy of not throwing anything away, were able to reuse various clips and snippets from the outtakes. These included, most significantly, Rick Wright's "Violent Sequence" (intended to back news footage of actual student riots), which would later feature as "Us and Them" on 1973's *The Dark Side of the Moon*.

## Touring

Early in January 1970, the band began a short tour of the UK and France, which included a broadcast on French radio recorded at the Théâtre des Champs-Élysées in Paris. Finishing at Leeds University at the end of February, the set list included a very preliminary version of an extended piece that would later be known as "Atom Heart Mother," the title track of their next album. And right after the conclusion of the tour, they began recording sessions at Abbey Road for what would be that fifth studio album.

Immediately prior to those first sessions, which commenced at the beginning of March, Rick Wright and David Gilmour had been in the studio to assist Syd Barrett on his second solo album.

The ex-Floyd man's first, *The Madcap Laughs*—with Gilmour and Roger Waters helping out on production—had just been released on January 2, but would fail to make any big impression on the charts, appearing at the No. 40 position for just one week. The new collection, simply titled *Barrett*, would fare no better sales-wise when it was released in November. Gilmour and Wright were named as producers, as well as contributing on a variety of instruments.

Recording the new Pink Floyd album was something of an on-off affair as the studio sessions had to be scattered within a hectic touring schedule that never seemed to let up for more than a day or so. After a BBC TV session on March 6, for the prestigious arts program *Line-Up* which aired a week later, Pink Floyd were back on the road with a string of European dates that took in Germany, Sweden, and Denmark, ending on the last day of the month in France.

A week later they were back in the United States for their third American tour. An array of prestigious venues, which were almost mandatory stop-offs for any visiting UK band, included the Fillmore East in New York City, the Fillmore West in San Francisco, and now-legendary spots including the Boston Tea Party, the Electric Ballroom in Philadelphia, and the Warehouse in New Orleans. This last venue signaled a premature end to the tour, with two Texas dates in Houston and Dallas being cancelled, after the theft of a large amount of their equipment in New Orleans.

The gear was stolen from a rental truck parked outside the Royal Orleans Hotel, where they were staying. As related in Nick Mason's 2004 history of the group, all the equipment less just two guitars magically reappeared a day or so later, after some behind-the-scenes cooperation from the local police. They

OPPOSITE: Actress Daria Halprin sitting on the shoulders of actor Mark Frechette during filming of *Zabriskie Point*, 1970

ABOVE: Italian director Michelangelo Antonioni (far right) on the set of *Zabriskie Point*

PAGES 74-75: Pink Floyd sitting on the stage at the Théâtre des Champs-Élysées, Paris, January 23, 1970

nevertheless decided not to reinstate the cancelled gigs and to return to England. A highlight of the trek, from the band's point of view, was an hour-long performance at the Fillmore West being filmed for a PBS TV broadcast as "An Hour with Pink Floyd."

Once back in the UK, the band were ready to premiere some of the music they had been preparing intermittently in the studio over the previous few months. The first date where the new Pink Floyd material was debuted was on June 27 at the Bath Festival of Blues and Progressive Music—formerly the Bath Blues Festival—in Shepton Mallet, Somerset. The two-day spectacular featured an impressive line-up that included top American acts including Santana, Canned Heat, and The Byrds, and top UK names like John Mayall and Led Zeppelin. Pink Floyd appeared at three in the morning on the Sunday, after some severe delays—they had originally been scheduled for 10.30 pm on the Saturday evening. Introduced to the audience under the title "The Amazing Pudding," the long set-piece (which would later become "Atom Heart Mother") was augmented by The John Aldiss Choir and The Philip Jones Brass Ensemble.

They repeated the exercise with the full line-up in London on July 18, when the band's ex-managers, Peter Jenner and Andrew King, staged the "Lose Your Head at Hyde Park" free concert, under the banner of Blackhill Enterprises. Headlining a bill that included Roy Harper, The Edgar Broughton Band, and Kevin Ayers, Pink Floyd were again joined by The Philip Jones Brass Ensemble and The John Aldiss Choir for "Atom Heart Mother." The augmentation of thirty extra musicians and singers was not to everyone's liking, however, with a *Melody Maker* review concluding "For their last number, 'Atom Heart Mother'—an electric symphony—they were joined by a 20-strong chorus and ten brass. The piece, which seemed to go on for eternity, was scratchy, and unfortunately the freelance musicians put nothing into it."

## Ron Geesin

Work on the centerpiece of the new album, the six-part title track that took up the whole of the first side, had actually begun soon after the band had returned from Rome after working on the *Zabriskie Point* soundtrack. Early elements of the piece had been aired during their brief tour of the UK and France in January and February, and would crop up in a gradually developed format at live gigs throughout the first half of the year—culminating in the Bath Blues Festival and Hyde Park concert, in June and July.

A major element in the development of "Atom Heart Mother" was the role of Ron Geesin, a musician, composer, and poet, who first came into the orbit of Pink Floyd via Nick

Mason a year or so earlier. As well as a talented composer and arranger, Geesin was also an innovative sound engineer, with a home studio full of electronic gadgetry. When Nick introduced him to Roger Waters in 1969, the two immediately hit it off, with Roger soon collaborating with Ron on the soundtrack of a film documentary, *The Body*.

Based on a book of the same name by Anthony Smith, the film—narrated by actors Vanessa Redgrave and Frank Finlay—was described by more than one reviewer as a movie version of a biology textbook. The soundtrack featured instrumental passages written by Geesin for cello, violin, and piano, four numbers sung by Waters, some sound-effect collaborations, and an uncredited contribution by the full Pink Floyd line-up on one song, "Give Birth to a Smile." The film was released in October 1970, followed by a soundtrack album in November.

Following their work on *The Body*, it came as no surprise that Roger would invite Ron Geesin to work on the next Pink Floyd album. While the band had been trying out various bits and pieces on the road, particularly the genesis of the title track which they had dubbed "The Amazing Pudding," it was nowhere near completion when they set off on their third American tour in April. So, with only a rough idea of what they wanted, but agreed on the notion of augmenting the title track with a choir and instrumental section (inspired by their Albert Hall concert in June 1969), they left the project in the hands of Geesin.

According to Geesin, apart from Roger Waters' suggestions, all he had to go on were some informal proposals from Rick, and a scribbled note of ideas for a

theme from David Gilmour. Nevertheless, on the band's return, Geesin presented them with a score which involved a ten-piece brass section, a twenty-piece choir, and solo cello arrangements. Studio time was subsequently booked at Abbey Road, but dealing with the in-house EMI session players—all hard-nosed professional classical players, unsympathetic to "amateur" rock musicians—proved difficult for Geesin. Ron contacted John Aldiss, a top-flight conductor and choirmaster who had plenty of experience in dealing with orchestral musicians, and whose choir proved ideal for the exercise.

## The Album

Ambitious in its concept, though more modest in its actual execution, the twenty-three-minute-plus title side of the album was presented as an instrumental "suite" with six separate sections. The main theme and "overture" of the piece was a direct result of the thematic suggestions of David Gilmour, recalling initially the grand vistas of epic Western films like *The Big Country* and the "spaghetti Western" concertos of Ennio Morricone. Indeed, an early working title when originally conceived by Gilmour was "Theme from an Imaginary Western."

The opening section, subtitled "Father's Shout," establishes the main theme splendidly with the aid of the brass players, before moving through "Breast Milky," which introduces the choir. The voices rise to a crescendo in the third phase, "Mother Fore," when something of a jam session ensues with "Funky Dung," bringing a more blues-tinged edge to the proceedings—especially in Gilmour's guitar solo, set against some repetitive keyboard motifs from Rick Wright. "Mind Your Throats Please" takes us into more electronic territory, before a sound-effects recording of a steam train transports the listener to a cacophony of various instrumental textures, as a disembodied voice shouts "Silence in the studio." The finale, "Remergence," thus announced, comprises the "Father's Shout" theme grandly reprised, culminating with the full choir and brass ensemble.

The second side of the album opens at a far more conventional pitch, with a Roger Waters song which in texture and vocal delivery sounds like an echo of his pastoral "Grantchester Meadows" from the band's previous *Ummagumma* collection. The lyrics of "If," however, have a far darker edge to them, as Waters indulges in a series of contradictions that hint at self-doubt rather than certainty.

Rick Wright's solo contribution continues things in a more mainstream vein than the first side's indulgences. Reminiscing on a brief romantic liaison, "Summer '68" is a beautifully crafted love song, embellished by a brass section that lifts the track to the level of near-perfect pop. Similarly, David Gilmour presses the nostalgia button in "Fat Old Sun," a gentle ballad that has the distinct feel of McCartney at his most wistful—although the strident guitar conclusion

hints at the flamboyant, lengthy ride-out that would characterize the song in the live concert version.

Back in their trademark territory of instrumental meanderings juxtaposed with various sound effects and electronic invention, the final track was ostensibly the "Nick Mason" track, though credited to the entire band. The subject matter, for want of a better description, was one of their roadies, Alan Styles, preparing and enjoying his breakfast—the title, "Alan's Psychedelic Breakfast," said it all. The thirteen-minute three-parter follows Styles's progress through his *petit déjeuner*, punctuated by snatches of his own commentary, sizzling bacon and eggs, and improvised doodling from the musicians. David Gilmour would later describe the track as "the most thrown-together thing we've ever done."

The band were at a loss for a title for the album. Eventually, at the suggestion of DJ John Peel, they randomly scoured a newspaper—the London *Evening Standard*—for a likely title, and came up with *Atom Heart Mother*, from a headline about a woman whose heart condition was being aided by a nuclear-powered pacemaker. And the title was also used for the album's opening, side-long track, previously known as "The Amazing Pudding."

# "If Pink Floyd is looking for some new dimensions, they haven't found them here."

## *Rolling Stone*

Once again, Pink Floyd went to their old friends at Hipgnosis for an album cover. They told Storm Thorgerson that they wanted something very simple on the sleeve, to deliberately get away from the psychedelics of previous artwork, and the photographic trickery of *Ummagumma*. Thorgerson, apparently inspired by Andy Warhol's iconic cow imagery on wallpaper, went out into the countryside outside London and photographed the first cow he came across. The cow, a Holstein-Friesian by the name of Lulubelle III, became an instant rock icon when John Peel urged his radio audience: "If you see an album featuring a nice picture of a cow, buy it immediately."

Released on October 2, 1970 in the UK, and a week later in America, *Atom Heart Mother* met with a mixed critical reception, although record buyers' reactions were far more positive. It was the band's biggest seller yet, hitting the No. 1 spot in the UK album charts, and No. 55 in the States. *Beat Instrumental* applauded "an utterly fantastic record that moves Floyd into new ground," and in the United States *Circus* magazine called it "trip trip trip, a tippy top trip," while *Rolling Stone*, on the other hand, concluded: "If Pink Floyd is looking for some new dimensions, they haven't found them here."

And the band themselves, though (naturally) enthusing about the album on its release, would be less than complimentary in years to come, with David Gilmour telling *Mojo* magazine in 2001: "*Atom Heart Mother* was a good idea, but it was dreadful. I listened to that album recently: God, it's shit, possibly our lowest point artistically. It sounds like we didn't have any idea between us, but we became much more prolific after it."

There was an interesting postscript to the release of the album, when the distinguished film director Stanley Kubrick expressed an interest in using the "Atom Heart Mother" title track in his upcoming movie, the dystopian drama *A Clockwork Orange*. The band were initially very keen on the idea, with Kubrick being one of the leading creative forces in international cinema at the time, but eventually turned down the idea—mainly on Roger Waters' insistence—when it transpired the director wanted freedom to edit the recording as he pleased. Nevertheless, the album was clearly visible behind the counter in a record store scene of the film, shot in the then-trendy Chelsea Drug Store (now a McDonald's) in London's King's Road.

OPPOSITE: Roger Waters pictured backstage at the Hakone Aphrodite concert, Japan, August 6, 1971

# Atom Heart Mother

Track Listing (original UK vinyl release)

**Side One**

Atom Heart Mother (Nick Mason, Roger Waters,
    Richard Wright, David Gilmour, Ron Geesin)
    I. Father's Shout
    II. Breast Milky
    III. Mother Fore
    IV. Funky Dung
    V. Mind Your Throats Please
    VI. Remergence

**Side Two**

If (Waters)
Summer '68 (Wright)
Fat Old Sun (Gilmour)
Alan's Psychedelic Breakfast (Waters, Mason, Gilmour,
    Wright)
    I. Rise and Shine
    II. Sunny Side Up
    III. Morning Glory

| | |
|---|---|
| **Recorded:** | March 1 – July 26, 1970, EMI Studios, Abbey Road, London |
| **Released:** | October 2, 1970 (UK), October 10, 1970 (US) |
| **Label:** | Harvest |
| **Producer:** | Pink Floyd |
| **Personnel:** | David Gilmour (guitars, vocals), Roger Waters (bass guitar, vocals), Richard Wright (keyboards, vocals), Nick Mason (drums) |
| **Additional Personnel:** | |
| | EMI Pops Orchestra, John Aldiss Choir, Hafliði Hallgrímsson (uncredited cello), Alan Styles (uncredited voice, sound effects) |
| **Chart Position:** | UK No. 1, US No. 55, France No. 4, Netherlands No. 5, Germany No. 8, Denmark No. 8, Italy No. 9 |

# meddle

"Anytime that anyone had any sort of rough idea of something we would put it down. At the end of January we listened back and we'd got 36 different bits and pieces that sometimes cross related and sometimes didn't."

### Nick Mason

OPPOSITE: Pink Floyd. L-R: Rick Wright, Roger Waters, Nick Mason, and David Gilmour photographed on Wimbledon Common, London, February 1971

## Juggling

The release of *Atom Heart Mother* at the beginning of October 1970 punctuated what seemed like a never-ending tour for Pink Floyd. Through the late summer the band had played various festivals in France including the International Jazz Festival in Antibes, the Festival International de Saint-Tropez, and the Pop Festival Saint-Raphaël. Then, to start their Atom Heart Mother world tour, they appeared at the Fête de l'Humanité, at the Bois de Vincennes in Paris, before setting off on their fourth North American tour. From Philadelphia at the end of September to Boston a month later, the band criss-crossed the US and Canada—after which most of November was taken up with an equally grueling schedule of dates across Europe. And the preparation and recording of their next album would similarly be something of a series of interruptions in a continuing datebook of gigs, through to its eventual release in October 1971.

The first month of the new year did, however, afford the band a breathing space between live performances, with just two appearances—at London's Roundhouse and Leeds University—in all of January. So with the welcome break from the road, they turned their attention once again to the recording studio. Initially, EMI's

Abbey Road was the obvious studio of choice for Pink Floyd, until they heard about the new sixteen-track tape machines being employed by ex-Beatles producer George Martin, at his own AIR Studios—an innovation the naturally conservative EMI had yet to embrace. The majority of the new album was subsequently recorded at Martin's state-of-the-art set-up in London's Oxford Street, with some additional finishes being made at Morgan Studios in the north-west London suburb of Willesden. And when the band resumed their hectic timetable of live concerts in February, it meant that the recording from start to finish would eventually last until September.

Meanwhile, as the band juggled studio time with their crowded diary of gig dates, the record company—concerned that Pink Floyd appeared to be making little progress on completing a new album in the near future—decided to release what was a traditional record industry stop-gap, a compilation of "oldies and goldies." Subtitled "A Bizarre Collection of Antiques and Curios," *Relics* hit the shops in May on EMI's

budget label Starline (and later Music for Pleasure). It was a mixed bag of oldies and album tracks, with the only "goldies" being the band's two most successful singles, "See Emily Play" and "Arnold Layne" from Barrett-era 1967. Alongside some long-forgotten B-sides—Rick Wright's "Paint Box," and David Gilmour's lead vocal debut on "Julia Dream" standing out—there was one unreleased song, "Biding My Time," a bluesy number notable for a trombone solo from Rick Wright.

On May 15, the day after the UK release of *Relics* (which for a compilation did well in getting to No. 32 in the album charts), the band topped the bill at the "Garden Party"—the first in a series of such presentations—at London's Crystal Palace Bowl. The line-up for the one-day mini-festival also featured Quiver, American heavy rock pioneers Mountain, and The Faces, but as it was a daytime event there was no need for the Floyd's flamboyant light show when the band closed the concert. Nevertheless, for Crystal Palace they planned one of their most spectacular performances yet.

Combined with a quadraphonic sound system and exploding smoke bombs, they had planned for a giant inflatable octopus to rise out of the ornamental lake in front of the stage when their set concluded with "A Saucerful of Secrets." In the event, the impact of the spectacle was dampened somewhat when over-enthusiastic fans leapt into the water and got caught up in the creature's tentacles, requiring a roadie to jump into the lake to untangle things. And the combination of dry ice, explosions, and ear-shattering volume during Pink Floyd's set was also blamed for the large number of fish that were found dead in the lake after the performance.

Plus, the weather didn't help, though the majority of the audience of fifteen thousand didn't seem to care when a torrential rainstorm of Biblical proportions

OPPOSITE: Crowds at the garden party, Crystal Palace Bowl, London, May 15, 1971

ABOVE: Nick Mason and Roger Waters perform live onstage with Pink Floyd at KB Hallen on September 23, 1971, Copenhagen, Denmark

"All of a sudden the sky cracked, and amazing fork lightning streaked straight across the back of the stage, with a tremendous boom . . . I am totally convinced the hippies thought it was part of the act."

**Eyewitness**

began just as Pink Floyd went onstage, as one eyewitness would graphically describe: "All of a sudden the sky cracked, and amazing fork lightning streaked straight across the back of the stage, with a tremendous boom, that made everyone jump and cheer. I am totally convinced the hippies thought it was part of the act. Then the heavens really opened up, and rain fell like an Indian monsoon. It just kept pouring and pouring down in dead straight lines. You could see no more than ten feet in front of yourself. Everyone pulled blankets and pieces of plastic over themselves to stop the downpour."

Through the rest of May and into the early summer there seemed hardly any let-up to the UK and European touring, with dates around England and Scotland followed by gigs in Germany, France, Italy, the Netherlands, and Austria. Then after a three-week break (though hardly a break, as they were catching up with the still-underdeveloped recording for a new album), in August '71 they made their first visit to Japan, followed by two dates in Australia.

The Japanese visit only amounted to three concerts, two at the Aphrodite Open Air Festival in Hakone, and one in Osaka. But during their brief sojourn the band also managed to take in some of the rich atmosphere of the country, with ancient temples and tranquil rock gardens contrasting with the high-tech vitality of its ultra-modern cities.

Although there were only two concerts in the band's debut visit to Australia, in Melbourne and Sydney, the trip was memorable in that it was when Pink Floyd met surf pioneer

> **"We may have agreed a basic chord structure but the tempo was random... These sound notes were called 'Nothings 1–24,' and the choice of name was apt."**
>
> **Nick Mason**

George Greenough for the first time. American surfer and cameraman Greenough was in the middle of writing and shooting a documentary film about surfing—something of a national sport in Australia—and showed the band some footage he'd already prepared. They were amazed; Greenough had developed a technique whereby a camera was strapped to a surfer's body (usually his own) to capture images from inside the "curl" of a wave, and he was searching for suitable music to accompany the slow-motion segment, as the final portion of the film.

The band agreed to providing music for the documentary, *Crystal Voyager*, in return for their being able to use portions of the footage as a backdrop in their live shows. The film, which would eventually be released in December 1973, featured the Pink Floyd music "Echoes," the twenty-three-minute sequence which would form the entire second side of the album they were currently completing between their touring commitments.

## Echoes

"Echoes" was the product of what had initially been a "writer's block" period in the recording studio, when the band spent what time they had between gigs producing literally nothing. With no new songs in the pipeline, and without a plan as to what they were aiming at, the four embarked on a series of experiments, including twenty minutes using the sound of everyday objects such as elastic bands, cigarette lighters, and wine bottles. The band dubbed the recordings *Household Objects*, though the album was never released.

Then they tried the idea of each member playing on separate recording tracks without reference to what the others were doing. Nick Mason would describe the process: "We may have agreed a basic chord structure but the tempo was random . . . These sound notes were called 'Nothings 1–24,' and the choice of name was apt." This and similar dead-ends ("Son of Nothings," "Return of the Son of Nothings") characterized several weeks of musical meandering, with an increasingly frustrated sound engineer, John Leckie, at the helm. Leckie would recall: "They were often going off to play gigs, so you'd have to strip down the studio, they'd load the van and go off and play a gig, then come back and set it

OPPOSITE: Rick Wright during a Pink Floyd concert, June 16, 1971, Abbey of Royaumont, France

ABOVE: Pink Floyd, June 1971, Germany

all up again." But ultimately, portions of what seemed a futile exercise morphed into a recognizably connected piece.

Later, Nick Mason would tell the *New Musical Express*: "'Echoes' was a specific attempt to sort of do something by a slightly different method. What we did, in fact, was book a studio for January; and throughout January we went in and played. Anytime that anyone had any sort of rough idea of something we would put it down. At the end of January we listened back and we'd got 36 different bits and pieces that sometimes cross related and sometimes didn't. 'Echoes' was made up from that."

A key element in the final mix was after Rick Wright put a single note on his piano through a rotating Leslie speaker to startling effect, achieving a sound not unlike the sonar "ping" associated with submarines. Despite the finished work's prodigious length, that simple repeated note—used as a marker at the beginning, two-thirds of the way through, and finale—gives the overall piece, and its varied constituents, a firm identity.

After Gilmour and Wright's delicate but brief harmony voicing of Waters' lyrics, "Echoes" progresses as a Pink Floyd tour de force—but without the guitar-heavy bombast that Floyd-influenced contemporaries of the time would usually bring to their own indulgences. Born out of a disparate collection of experiments in recorded sound, the track has since been hailed as a milestone in the band's development, as marking a point between their status as an inventive cult band with a substantial global following, and genuine mainstream superstars.

"Echoes"—which they all agreed was a better name than the working title "Return of the Son of Nothings"—undoubtedly inspired a fresh burst of creativity in the studio. The second-side epic was preceded on the album—to be titled *Meddle*—by a collection of half a dozen more conventional tracks, beginning with the mainly instrumental "One of These Days," which opens with a strident, one-note bass line that is actually Waters and Gilmour in unison, recorded as one musician for each stereo channel. The sparse lyrics—just twelve words in all—are delivered by Nick Mason taped at double speed, then replayed at normal speed. With Gilmour's blistering guitar riding things out, it would be an inevitable crowd-pleaser.

LEFT: Pink Floyd, 1971

PAGES 94-95: Rick Wright and David Gilmour at a press conference, Hakone Aphrodite, Tokyo, Japan, August 2, 1971

The dreamy Waters and Gilmour composition "A Pillow of Winds" sinks lazily into the acoustic territory occupied by the likes of Crosby, Stills & Nash. The title originates in the traditional Chinese game of mah-jongg, which the band were keen on playing. "Fearless" is another easy-on-the-ear offering; with a lead vocal by Gilmour, interest is heightened by the fade-out inclusion of the crowd at Liverpool Football Club singing their iconic anthem "You'll Never Walk Alone." Rick Wright would explain the context of the stadium recording to (presumably soccer-ignorant) listeners on a local American radio station: "It's called 'The Kop Choir.' And they just never stop singing throughout the whole match, and it's, in fact,

BELOW: Pink Floyd original vinyl album internal sleeve for *Meddle*, 1971

much more incredible than it sounds on that record. Because you just wouldn't believe how loud it is from the start. I mean, we couldn't compete with a hundred-thousand voice choir."

The final two tracks on the top side of the album are decidedly lightweight, especially considering the mammoth work rolled out on Side Two. "San Tropez," a jazz-tinged piece referencing a trip to the South of France the band had made the previous summer, was written by Waters, who delivers the vocal in an easy-going manner that he was becoming increasingly adept at. And "Seamus," a quasi-blues, is remarkable in that David Gilmour's lead vocal is backed by the energetic howling of a dog, the eponymous Seamus. The border collie had been trained by its

owner, singer Steve Marriott, to accompany the sound of a blues harp, and here backs Gilmour's vamping with gusto.

*Meddle* was released at the end of October in the US, and a week later in the UK, failing to do well in the former territory (a meager No. 70 in the LP chart) but achieving a very respectable No. 3 on their home ground. The failure to achieve bigger sales in America was put down partly to a lack of enthusiasm on the part of their US record company's publicity machine (although they did sell nearly a quarter of a million copies). But the band recognized they had yet to conquer the transatlantic market properly, as Nick Mason would confirm: "In America, for instance, we've still got a lot of work to do. There's still

**"In America, for instance, we've still got a lot of work to do. There's still very few bands who can command any price. Any other place in the world we can ask our price but only every so often."**

**Nick Mason**

very few bands who can command any price. Any other place in the world we can ask our price but only every so often." On its release, the album received generally better notices than its immediate predecessor. *Rolling Stone*'s Jean-Charles Costa concluded his review: "*Meddle* is killer Floyd from start to finish," while Ed Kelleher writing in *Circus* judged it "another masterpiece by a masterful group."

One issue that most fans and music pundits seemed to agree on was disappointment with the album cover design by Hipgnosis. Following the enigmatic images that made the sleeve art of both *Ummagumma* and *Atom Heart Mother* memorable, the blurry picture on the cover of *Meddle* seemed to come as something of an anti-climax. The story goes that Storm Thorgerson had suggested a close-up photograph of a baboon's backside, but the band—apparently inspired by the spiritual quality of Japanese water gardens—requested a picture of a human ear under water, with the ripples representing waves of sound. Photographer Bob Dowling captured an image that followed their wishes, but was so close-up that it appeared to be more abstract than realistic. Boring perhaps, but for better or worse it was certainly less controversial than a baboon's bottom!

OPPOSITE: David Gilmour, June 16, 1971, Abbey of Royaumont, France

# Meddle

Track Listing (original UK vinyl release)

### Side One
One of These Days (David Gilmour, Roger Waters, Richard Wright, Nick Mason)
A Pillow of Winds (Waters, Gilmour)
Fearless (including "You'll Never Walk Alone") (Waters, Gilmour plus Richard Rodgers and Oscar Hammerstein II)
San Tropez (Waters)
Seamus (Waters, Wright, Mason, Gilmour)

### Side Two
Echoes (Waters, Wright, Mason, Gilmour)

**Recorded:** January 4 – September 11, 1971, AIR Studios, London; EMI Studios, London; Morgan Studios, London

**Released:** October 30, 1971 (US), November 5, 1971 (UK)

**Label:** Harvest

**Producer:** Pink Floyd

**Personnel:** David Gilmour (guitars, bass guitar, harmonica, vocals), Roger Waters (bass guitar, guitar, vocals), Richard Wright (keyboards, vocals), Nick Mason (drums, percussion, vocals)

**Additional Personnel:** Seamus the dog (vocals)

**Chart Position:** UK No. 3, US No. 70, Belgium No. 10, Netherlands No. 2, Denmark No. 6, Italy No. 11

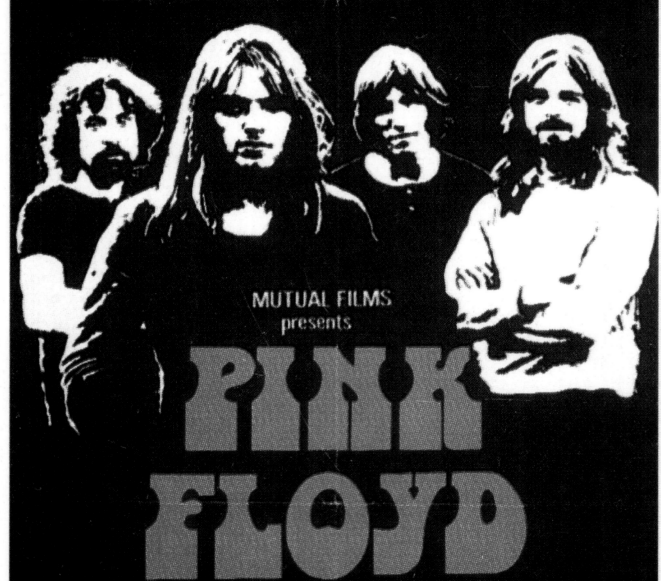

"A STUNNING AUDIO-VISUAL EXPERIENCE." — VARILTY

AT LAST THE ROCK WIZARDS ARE UNLEASHED ON FILM

MUTUAL FILMS
presents

PINK
FLOYD

"GOES BEYOND PERFECTION."
CASH BOX

"A ZAPPAESQUE MUSICAL PASTICHE."
MELODY MAKER

# obscured by clouds

"Audiences are a bit divided
between getting bored
with old numbers after
reliving their childhood,
or reliving their golden
era of psychedelia."

## Nick Mason

# Pompeii

**P**rior to the release of *Meddle*, at the beginning of October 1971 Pink Floyd embarked on yet another side-project interrupting the usual rock routine of touring and recording. The band had been approached by the film director Adrian Maben with the idea of shooting them in performance, but instead of in front of a conventional rock concert audience, it would be with virtually no onlookers at all, in an ancient Roman amphitheater in the ruins of Pompeii. Maben's idea was to get away from the usual conventions of rock concert movies, as most famously typified in D. A. Pennebaker's *Monterey Pop* (released in 1968) and Michael Wadleigh's *Woodstock* from two years later.

So the band took off for Italy, and after three days of delays involving a lack of electricity, played live (they insisted on no miming) as if to an audience, under the shadow of Mount Vesuvius. Intercut with shots of the volcano's steaming lava flowing across the rugged landscape, the band performed the yet-to-be-released "Echoes" and "One of These Days" from *Meddle*, alongside various older favorites including "A Saucerful of Secrets." The local town council gave permission for the site—normally a popular tourist attraction—to be closed for a week for the filming. The only audience were the crew, a few Floyd hangers-on, and some local children who managed to sneak in.

Additional sessions were included in the film, shot in Paris at the Studio Europasonor through the week of December 13. The studio sequences included

OPPOSITE: Movie still from *Pink Floyd: Live at Pompeii*, 1972

BELOW L-R: Film director Adrian Maben, Rick Wright, David Gilmour, Nick Mason, and Roger Waters during the filming of *Live at Pompeii* at Studio Europa Sonor in Paris, France, December 1971

"Set the Controls for the Heart of the Sun," "Careful with That Axe, Eugene," and bizarrely a reworking of "Seamus" from *Meddle*, with a dog called Nobs credited as Mademoiselle Nobs.

*Pink Floyd: Live at Pompeii*, or at least a truncated version of it, premiered at the Edinburgh International Film Festival in September 1972. Running for just over an hour, this cut featured only the live footage of the band, while a later release first shown in Montreal, Canada, in November 1973, ran to eighty minutes. Including extra studio sequences shot at Abbey Road earlier that year, this was the "official" version that would eventually be released in the US and elsewhere in the summer of 1974. By that time, of course, the film had a certain dated look about it—especially in the context of it being eclipsed by their biggest success yet, *The Dark Side of the Moon*, which would appear in March 1973.

Probably for that reason, there was never a soundtrack album released along with the movie, although in 2017 David Gilmour would release *Live at Pompeii*, coinciding with a cinema film of the same title. Shot at the same amphitheater venue, the album and movie were recorded and filmed in 2016, during the guitarist's solo world tour promoting his 2015 album *Rattle That Lock*.

## La Vallée

With the (welcome) distraction of filming and recording *Pompeii* behind them, the opening weeks of 1972 saw the band addressing more immediate matters at hand, namely thinking about their next album. After two weeks of preparation in The Rolling Stones' rehearsal facility in south London, the band played sixteen dates around the UK performing what they would describe as "in progress" versions of their next album project, *The Dark Side of the Moon*. The tour culminated in a "press preview" of the work, at the time called *Dark Side of the Moon: A Piece for Assorted Lunatics*, over a year before its actual release on record.

As Nick Mason would explain in a press interview, there was always a tension between whether to give audiences the "oldies" they obviously wanted to hear, or a taste of intriguing things to come. "Audiences are a bit divided between getting bored with old numbers after reliving their childhood, or re-living their golden era of psychedelia, or even wanting to hear what it was all about. These are OK reasons for wanting to hear something but they aren't very valid for us."

And again, Pink Floyd were happy to be interrupted by what they perceived as more "artistic" endeavors, when they were

ABOVE: Recording *Pink Floyd: Live at Pompeii*, 1972

offered another soundtrack project by Barbet Schroeder, who they had worked with in 1969 on his film *More*. So preparation for *Dark Side* was postponed while the band repaired to Strawberry Studios in the elegant Château d'Hérouville outside Paris. Built in 1740, the thirty-room mansion was converted into residential recording studios in 1969, and gained fame after Elton John recorded his *Honky Château* there in January 1972, just a few weeks prior to Pink Floyd booking in. During that first week at the Château, a short segment of the group recording was filmed for the French national TV station ORTF, and included interviews with both Roger Waters and David Gilmour.

PINK
FLOYD.
LONDON

## "We only had two weeks to record the soundtrack with a short amount of time afterwards to turn it into an album."

### Nick Mason

people, the Mapuga, whose primitive lifestyle inspires the idealistic Westerners to emulate them.

As with their previous cinematic collaboration with Schroeder, the group employed the same system of using stopwatches to establish musical cues while viewing a rough cut of the film. And again the director utilized much of the band's contribution as "source music," emanating from a radio or suchlike in an actual scene, rather than as a conventional background soundtrack. Hence the band came up with a series of short, straightforward songs, rather than the inspired musical explorations they were now mainly associated with.

Time was also of the essence: "We had no scope for self-indulgence," Nick Mason would recall. "We only had two weeks to record the soundtrack with a short amount of time afterwards to turn it into an album." Those two weeks at the Château—the last week in February and four or five days at the end of March—were either side of a whistle-stop tour of Japan. The band completed mixing the soundtrack in early April at London's Morgan Studios, for an album release date in early June. By that time, however, after some disagreements with the film company, the band had altered the album title from *La Vallée* to *Obscured by Clouds*. The film went on to be released in cinemas a month after the album, and the band were delighted when the film company decided to bill the movie as *La Vallée (Obscured by Clouds)* to tie in with (or cash in on?) the record.

## Obscured by Clouds

The most action-related sequence, where the music complemented what was happening on screen, came in the first minutes of the film—and the opening title track to the album—with the image of a light aircraft flying over the New Guinea rainforest. Richard Wright had just acquired a state-of-the-art VCS3 synthesizer (from the famous BBC Radiophonic Workshop) which was ideally suited to the scene, accompanied by Gilmour's fuzz-boxed guitar. From there on, however, much of the music seemed arbitrary to the action being played out in the movie.

Nevertheless, some of the songs, though they could be

The film itself, *La Vallée*, was very much in the countercultural narrative context of *More*, concerning a rich hippie, the unhappy wife of a French diplomat, who travels to Papua New Guinea to source rare birds' feathers for her Paris boutique. Once there the heroine Viviane—played by Schroeder's wife Bulle Ogier—soon gets caught up with like-minded hedonists, including the charismatic Olivier who is searching for a mythic valley ("La Vallée" of the film's title), marked on the map simply with the words "Obscured by Clouds." In their search for an imagined Paradise on Earth, the group encounter a tribe of indigenous

OPPOSITE: Bulle Ogier movie still from *La Vallée* (aka *The Valley Obscured by the Clouds*), 1972

ABOVE: Rick Wright, 1972

considered inconsequential compared to Pink Floyd's main canon of work, had value in their own right. There was a definite country feel to much of the album, exemplified in the loping soft-rocker "The Gold It's in the . . ." credited to Gilmour and Waters, while "Wot's . . . Uh, the Deal?" (also by the pair, who between them dominate the writer credits) has a vocal harmony texture reminiscent of *Abbey Road* Beatles.

By this stage in the group's development, Roger Waters' songwriting was often characterized by pessimistic "doom and gloom" sentiments, a trait that fitted the impression of many that he could be "difficult" to work with. In "Free Four"—despite its jaunty Cockney count-in "One, two, free, four . . ."—he manages to reference both his jaded view of the music industry, and the death of his father in World War II, the latter theme previously alluded to in "Corporal Clegg" from 1968's *Saucerful of Secrets*.

The track actually made it to a single release in the US, though failing to chart, with the album's penultimate song, "Stay," as the B-side. And the Mapuga tribe even made an appearance on the final track, with their ritual chanting on the otherwise instrumental ride-out "Absolutely Curtains."

Once again Storm Thorgerson and Aubrey Powell at Hipgnosis were responsible for the cover art, which like their work for its predecessor, *Meddle*, failed to have the impact promised by previous albums, from *A Saucerful of Secrets* to *Atom Heart Mother*. The picture was from *La Vallée*, and was derived from a 35 mm slideshow of stills that Storm and Aubrey were viewing when the projector jammed. The resulting blurry image, of one of the hippie explorers perched in a tree, was so distorted that it was virtually undistinguishable; nevertheless, the Hipgnosis pair decided that was what they wanted for the

album. As Thorgerson later wrote: "Suddenly, in front of our very eyes, the out-of-focus quality imbued an ordinary image with more transcendental qualities—or so we told Barbet." Much to the annoyance of Thorgerson and Powell, Barbet Schroeder later insisted that they deliberately chose an uninspired sleeve design, so as not to compete with Floyd's next major release—which in fact would be a full nine months after *Obscured by Clouds* hit the shops in June 1972.

Like Pink Floyd's earlier soundtrack album, the collection surprised some when it hit the UK charts at No. 6. Though not a lackluster release by any means, from the start the project had seemed to represent the group marking time before their next major enterprise in the recording studio. Reviews in the music press were mixed, some attesting that it identified Pink Floyd as a straight rock band rather than experimenters on the fringe of things. Tony Stewart boldly declared in the *New Musical Express*, "It's melodic even to the point of unabashed commercialism. Floyd come out as a rock band of some great appeal," concluding a laudatory (though not uncritical) review: "Despite some poor production work, this is a most satisfying, comprehensive album from Floyd. It shows that not only are they masters of their instruments, but also able song writers." And retrospective assessments likewise have often given the album the benefit of the doubt, as when the *Daily Telegraph*'s Neil McCormick wrote in 2014: "Its elegant instrumentals point the way to *Dark Side*."

OPPOSITE: Nick Mason, 1972

ABOVE: Roland Petit (left) with ballet dancers Margot Fonteyn and Rudolf Nureyev. Pink Floyd collaborated with choreographer Petit on a "Pink Floyd Ballet" staged in 1972. A movie version starring Nureyev was also discussed, but ultimately never materialized.

## Ballet de Marseille

Between *Obscured by Clouds* and their next album release, the band continued their usual gig-packed touring schedule. This included another North American tour (their seventh); three consecutive charity concerts for War on Want and Save the Children at London's Wembley Empire Pool in October 1972; more European dates before and after the New Year; and another US trek in March '73, that heralded the new album.

The European dates would include another artistic "distraction" from Floyd's usual performance schedule, when they accompanied choreographer Roland Petit's Ballet National de Marseille dance company. The band had first been approached by Petit in 1970, when he proposed they collaborate on a stage version of the epic novel by Marcel Proust, *À la recherche du temps perdu* (*In Search of Lost Time*). In order to get a feel for the gigantic work, it was suggested the band read the entire twelve volumes in preparation. In the event, they all gave up after a book or two (with Gilmour apparently managing just eighteen pages!), and the whole idea was abandoned.

Petit himself was not one to admit defeat, however, and in November 1972 he staged a production with the band involving a four-movement "Pink Floyd Ballet." The group played a sequence from their established repertoire—"One of These Days," "Careful with That Axe, Eugene," "Obscured by Clouds," "When You're In," and "Echoes"—and the novelty of being accompanied by a professional ballet company was a refreshing diversion. The shows were staged for five nights at the Salle Vallier in Marseille, and in January–February the exercise was repeated for four performances at the Palais des Sports de la Porte de Versailles, Paris.

The association with the refined world of ballet appealed to what Nick Mason would describe as "intellectual snobbery" on the part of the band—especially when back in London Roland Petit convened a lunch to discuss a film version of the Proust project. Nick, Roger, and manager Steve O'Rourke attended alongside Petit, ballet superstar Rudolf Nureyev, and film director Roman Polanski. There was also mention of a screen adaptation of the "Echoes" section of the Pink Floyd ballet, which was loosely based on Mary Shelley's *Frankenstein*. Nothing came of the lengthy lunchtime discussions, however, which as the Floyd contingent recalled, were memorable if only for the amount of wine consumed.

OPPOSITE: Roger Waters, 1972

# Obscured by Clouds

Track Listing (original UK vinyl release)

**Side One**
Obscured by Clouds (David Gilmour, Roger Waters)
When You're In (Gilmour, Waters, Richard Wright, Nick Mason)
Burning Bridges (Wright, Waters)
The Gold It's in the . . . (Gilmour, Waters)
Wot's . . . Uh the Deal? (Gilmour, Waters)
Mudmen (Wright, Gilmour)

**Side Two**
Childhood's End (Gilmour)
Free Four (Waters)
Stay (Wright, Waters)
Absolutely Curtains (Gilmour, Waters, Wright, Mason)

| | |
|---|---|
| **Recorded:** | February 23 – April 6, 1972, Strawberry Studios, Château d'Hérouville, France |
| **Released:** | June 2, 1972 (UK), June 17, 1972 (US) |
| **Label:** | Harvest |
| **Producer:** | Pink Floyd |
| **Personnel:** | David Gilmour (guitars, VCS3 synthesizer, vocals), Roger Waters (bass guitar, vocals), Richard Wright (keyboards, VCS3 synthesizer, vocals), Nick Mason (drums, percussion) |
| **Additional Personnel:** | Mapuga tribe |
| **Chart Position:** | UK No. 6, US No. 46, Denmark No. 3, Netherlands No. 3, Italy No. 5 |

# the dark side of the moon

"A lot of people, including engineers and roadies, when we asked them, didn't know what the LP was about. I really don't know if our things get through, but you have to carry on hoping."

**David Gilmour**

# Genesis

The genesis of Pink Floyd's next album, and their first non-soundtrack album since *Meddle* in 1971, flew in the face of rock music convention. Whereas normally a new release would be promoted by live dates immediately before, or soon after, an album's appearance in stores, the Floyd's successor to *Obscured by Clouds* was being previewed to audiences more than a year prior to its availability.

The closing weeks of 1971 had seen the band—not for the first time—in a state of acute indecision when it came to their next project in the recording studio. In order to accentuate the positive (to quote a 1940s pop song), Roger Waters convened a full meeting of the quartet at Nick Mason's home in Camden Town, London.

Despite a general lack of direction on the part of the other three, Waters had been busying himself writing lyrics, and at the get-together in Nick's kitchen

BELOW: Pink Floyd in concert at the Rainbow Theatre, London, 1972

laid out his ideas for their next venture. His rationale was that, with UK gigs coming up in the New Year, one half of their stage repertoire could be enough new material to fill an album, with the second half of their show devoted to familiar songs. With that in mind, Roger suggested themes that were emerging in his latest batch of lyrics—significantly of mental disturbance, and associated social anxieties—that would form the basis for the new album. "At the start we only had vague ideas about madness being a theme," Richard Wright would recall. "We rehearsed a lot just putting down ideas, and then in the next rehearsals we used them."

At the end of November, the band booked time at Decca Studios in West Hampstead, London, where they began writing and laying down samples for the new project, with the working title of *Eclipse*. The band had already come up with *Dark Side of the Moon* (a reference to lunacy, not astronomy) as a provisional name, only to discover that the UK group Medicine Head had already released an album with the identical moniker. But when they discovered that the latter release hadn't sold at all well, Pink Floyd decided to revert to their original choice anyway.

After some additional filming and recording in Paris for their *Live at Pompeii* project, they were in rehearsals once again early in January, this time at The Rolling Stones' studio facility in south London, followed by onstage rehearsals at London's Rainbow Theatre. As part of Roger Waters' concept, these were primarily gig run-throughs for the presentation of their new material to concert audiences. Also with their

live performances in mind, the band had radically upgraded their PA system, which now included a twenty-eight-channel mixing desk with four-channel quadraphonic output, plus a new custom-built lighting system.

The first public performance of the new music was scheduled for January 20, 1972 at the Dome, Brighton, the first date on a sixteen-concert UK tour. Billed as "Dark Side of the Moon: A Piece for Assorted Lunatics," the piece had to be unceremoniously cut short, halfway through the song "Money," after some embarrassing technical problems. "Due to severe mechanical and electric horror we can't do any more of that bit . . ." Roger announced to a nonplussed crowd, ". . . so we'll do something else." The band then retired for a break, returning to complete the performance with some tried-and-trusted favorites including "Atom Heart Mother," "Echoes," and "A Saucerful of Secrets."

In the event, the audience gave them the benefit of the doubt, as did the man from *Melody Maker*: "What their music lacked in framework and conception it seemed to be trying to compensate for with volume and aural clarity. Even this produced its problems for the group, in that their speakers were cursed with breakdown and this undoubtedly affected the concert." And even Nick Mason, talking to the *New Musical Express* right after the concert, was making the best of a below-par job: "Frankly, I thought some of tonight was fantastic. Like there's all sorts of cueing things that we have to sort out, but the lighting system is amazing. It's a new start."

OPPOSITE: Nick Mason performs live onstage, London, 1972

ABOVE: Rick Wright backstage at Amsterdam Rock Circus, Olympisch Stadium, May 22, 1972, Netherlands

PAGES 118-119: David Gilmour and Nick Mason live onstage with Pink Floyd, at the Winter Gardens, Bournemouth, January 22, 1972

PAGES 120-121: Pink Floyd performing live onstage, circa 1972

The rest of the tour—not without a few more technical glitches—culminated in four nights at the Rainbow Theatre, the first on February 17 being an official "press preview" for the assembled music journalists. The album section of the show—with the songs performed in exactly the order they would eventually appear on the vinyl release—was received favorably by most of the scribes, with *The Times*' Michael Wale reporting the music as "bringing tears to the eyes. It was so completely understanding and musically questioning . . ."

Committing the set-piece of new material to studio masters would be put on hold. Just three days after the UK trek wound up at the Rainbow, the band were in France recording the *La Vallée* soundtrack at the Château d'Hérouville. Then they were on the road again, for a six-date tour of Japan on which they previewed *The Dark Side of the Moon* as part of every concert. The live performances in Japan, and subsequent tours of the US, UK, and Europe over the next few months, enabled Pink Floyd to gradually fine-tune the songs for the upcoming album, which some fans were beginning to think might never actually appear!

Finally, on May 24, 1972, the band began a month-long stint

> ## "Frankly, I thought some of tonight was fantastic. Like there's all sorts of cueing things that we have to sort out, but the lighting system is amazing. It's a new start."
>
> ## Nick Mason

of recording at the EMI studios in Abbey Road. At this stage, a number of the songs that would constitute *The Dark Side of the Moon* had temporary working titles, including "Travel" (that would later appear as "Breathe"), "Scat" (later "Any Colour You Like"), and "Religion" ("The Great Gig in the Sky"). And although some tracks laid down were virtually finished versions, the project as a whole was still very much a work in progress, the new songs still being crowd-tested as Pink Floyd resumed touring across Europe and America.

Any further recording at Abbey Road was interrupted by the band's enormous touring schedules, plus their extracurricular divergencies including Pompeii, the *La Vallée / Obscured by Clouds* soundtrack, and at the end of the year the Roland Petit ballet gigs. So opportunities for studio time between live dates were grabbed whenever possible, culminating in one final series of sessions at Abbey Road from January 9, 1973 to the first day in February.

## Recording

With the band themselves central to proceedings at the production desk, right from the first sessions in May '72 they were joined by Alan Parsons, a member of the Abbey Road in-house staff, as recording engineer. Parsons, whose résumé included work on The Beatles' *Abbey Road* and *Let It Be* albums, had already assisted with Pink Floyd as tape operator on *Atom Heart Mother* in 1970. With his expertise in the studio, having come up through EMI's apprentice system, Parsons proved an invaluable collaborator on Pink Floyd's latest project.

Despite the term being somewhat overused in the context of early-seventies "progressive" rock, *The Dark Side of the Moon* was very much a "concept" album. Each side of the vinyl long-player took the form of a continuous piece of music, physically joining together the variations on the general theme of the human condition. And, as was made apparent at that first collective meeting in November 1971, it was very much Roger Waters' concept from the start. Over thirty years later, Waters was happy to reaffirm that concept when interviewed in 2003: "You make choices during your life, and those choices are influenced by political considerations and by money and by the dark side of all our natures. You get the chance to make the world a lighter or a darker place in some small way."

For every track on the album, except three instrumentals, the lyrics were provided by Waters, a role that confirmed—for the time being at least—his status as the dominant creative force in the band.

Much of the music being recorded had its roots in the various experiments that characterized Pink Floyd's previous work onstage and in the studio, but pared down without the extended instrumental passages—which David Gilmour would later call "psychedelic noodling stuff"—that had become something of a trademark. Now the numbers were cleaner, more direct, benefitting from an element of self-discipline on the part of all four musicians. The album became the most celebrated in Pink Floyd's studio output, and over half a century later is worthy of a detailed assessment.

A continuous linkage is apparent from the very start of the album, when disembodied voices fade in to the background of a human heartbeat and the ticking of a watch. This was the listener's introduction to a Roger Waters brainchild that crops up throughout the work: the bassist posed fifteen questions, which he presented to various individuals including the road crew, EMI personnel, and others working in the studios, and recorded their answers. On the first track, "Speak to Me" / Breathe," we hear the Floyd roadie Chris Adamson and studio doorman Gerry O'Driscoll in a one-minute-plus sound collage, which was envisaged as an overture to the entire work, as Nick Mason would put it, "A taster of things to come." The "Breathe" section of the double track, with a languid vocal from Gilmour, introduced a novel device, a melody that would recur in different form after the next two songs, "On the Run" and "Time."

The instrumental "On the Run" represents a state-of-the art exercise in synth-based sound effects, addressing the pressures of travel, and the attendant horrors for those—like Rick Wright—with a fear of flying. As if awakening us from the paranoia lurking behind the perceived nightmare of air travel, a bedside alarm heralds "Time" with a cacophony of clock sounds, sourced by Alan Parsons. The sound engineer had recorded the myriad timepieces at an antique watchmaker's shop a couple of months earlier, for a demonstration record

of quadraphonic effects. The strident vocals, shared by Gilmour and Wright, relate Waters' realization in his late twenties that he was no longer preparing for life, but was enacting it in the here and now. As he explained to *Mojo* magazine in 1998: "I suddenly thought, at 29, 'Hang on, it's happening, it has been right from the beginning,' and there isn't suddenly a line where the training stops and life starts." "Time" is the first track to feature the four backing vocalists who appear on the album, Doris Troy, Lesley Duncan, Liza Strike, and Barry St. John, all time-served session singers.

The other additional vocal contributor to the album appears on "The Great Gig in the Sky," the iconic final track of Side One on the vinyl pressing. Clare Torry was an experienced session singer and solo voice in her own right, well known to Alan Parsons through her frequent work at Abbey Road, often involved in compilation albums of covers of popular hits. When she discussed the proposed track with Pink Floyd, the band were particularly vague as to what was wanted, telling her there were no words or melody to follow, just a chord sequence. As Torry would later recall, "They told me what the album was about: birth and death, and everything in between. I thought it was rather pretentious, to be honest."

After listening to the instrumental track that the four had already recorded, and without any firm direction as to what they expected of her, she decided: "Maybe I should just pretend I'm

> ## "I suddenly thought, at 29, 'Hang on, it's happening, it has been right from the beginning,' and there isn't suddenly a line where the training stops and life starts."
> ### Roger Waters

an instrument." The result, after just two or three takes, was remarkable. With the theme written by Rick Wright, the pianist's stately intro, aided by David Gilmour's ghostly slide guitar, paints an evocative aural landscape over which Torry's abstract, wordless, but impassioned vocal takes us to unexpected, other-worldly places. Alongside "Money," which opened Side Two, it would become a trademark track for the entire album.

When the session was over, Torry was convinced that her contribution would probably not make the final cut for the album. It was only when she saw the record on sale in a local store, with her name on the personnel credits, that she realized it had, indeed, been used. She had been paid the standard session fee of £30 (the equivalent of less than £500 in the early 2020s), and when the album became one of the biggest sellers of all time, Torry (with some justification) decided she deserved a cut in the writers' royalties for her significant contribution to the actual composition. In 2004 the singer sued EMI and Pink Floyd, the case being settled out of court for an undisclosed sum, with her name featured on the composer credit, alongside Richard Wright, from there on.

With the chink of coins (achieved by some small change being tossed around in a bowl) and a cash register ringing, "Money" opens with a string of sound effects first spliced together by Roger Waters and Nick Mason, in Waters' garden-shed studio. The memorable bass-led intro lays the foundation for David Gilmour's sonorous delivery of Roger Waters' tirade against modern consumerism. Referencing caviar, buying a football club, Learjets, and other totems of conspicuous wealth, there was a certain irony in the lyrics when the song—and the album—went on to be a multi-million worldwide money-earner for Waters, and the rest of the band. And the instrumental passage at the center of the track was a milestone for Pink Floyd, with session saxophonist Dick Parry cutting through with a soul-drenched tenor break (despite the tricky 7/4 time signature) before Gilmour's guitar really tears things up ahead of the concluding vocals.

The fade-out segue includes some more of Waters' vox-pop recordings taped at Abbey Road, including the laconic voice—"I don't know, I was really drunk at the time"—of Henry McCullough, guitarist with Paul McCartney's Wings. It transpired that McCartney was working on his album *Red Rose Speedway* in an adjoining studio, and both he and wife Linda agreed to contribute an ad-lib to Roger Waters' questionnaire. Their particular responses, however, were never finally used.

The first track to be actually completed at Abbey Road was "Us and Them," on May 31, 1972, followed just a week later by "Money." Instrumentally, the song was based on a laid-back, economical piece by Rick Wright that had first emerged as an unused theme in the soundtrack work for *Zabriskie Point*. The lyrical feel of the vocal parts, voiced by Dave Gilmour and the four session singers, is contrasted

OPPOSITE: Nick Mason and Roger Waters perform live onstage with Pink Floyd, London, 1972

ABOVE: Singer Clare Torry pictured in 1969. In 2005, Torry received a retrospective credit for "vocal composition" on "The Great Gig in the Sky" after she sued EMI and Pink Floyd for songwriting royalties.

by the rich backing of Dick Parry's tenor saxophone. Subject-wise, it's another stab at putting the world to rights on the part of Roger Waters, or at least highlighting some of the attendant problems facing humanity. At nearly eight minutes, the longest track on the album, it's an inspiring piece that ranks among the band's most haunting studio achievements.

Although an instrumental track, "Any Colour You Like" is often perceived as another of Roger Waters' critiques of capitalism, this time implicit in the title. The root of the notion, that there are no real choices in society, goes back to the famous comment of industrialist Henry Ford, who said of his Model T automobile that you could have any color "as long as it's black." The relaxed interaction between Gilmour's Stratocaster guitar and Wright's VCS3 synth provides a cool intermission between the intensity of "Us and Them," and the stark psychic realities that follow in "Brain Damage."

Roger Waters had played an early rendering of "Brain Damage"

during the 1971 sessions for *Meddle*, when it was actually called "The Dark Side of the Moon," with the phrase appearing in the finished version in the line "I'll see you on the dark side of the moon." At one stage the band also referred to the still-to-be-finalized song as "Lunatic." Waters has stated categorically that the song was a reflection of the deteriorating mental state of their former colleague Syd Barrett, and in many ways it is a summing-up of the overriding theme of the whole album. Recorded in October 1972 at the same time as the preceding "Any Colour You Like," Waters' vocals were of the same folky flavor associated with earlier acoustic-based songs such as "Grantchester Meadows." Nevertheless, the soaring texture of Rick's Hammond organ, along with the four backing vocalists, lifts the track into altogether more soul-tinged territory.

The final track on the album, "Eclipse," sounds almost like a coda to the previous track. As Nick Mason would acknowledge, the piece had evolved via frequent live performances to the climactic level achieved in the studio: "The original versions . . . lacked any real dynamic, but with gradual development onstage—where we needed to end the piece on a grander note—it acquired sufficient power to make a suitable finale." And as if to tie things up completely, the album closes as it began—a human heartbeat, followed by the disembodied voice of studio employee Gerry O'Driscoll with a closing hint of melancholy: "There is no dark side of the moon, matter of fact, it's all dark."

## Release

The album was released in America on March 10, 1973, and in the UK on the 23rd. Although they were personally very enthusiastic about the whole project, the band were apprehensive as to the general reaction, both on the part of critics and fans. Regarding the coterie of UK music journalists, not all of whom were convinced Floyd fans by any means, EMI Records organized a press reception for the launch of the album at the London Planetarium. Dismayed at the label's perpetuating an association between themselves and outer space—a link mistakenly implied in the title of the LP—the band were dubious about the event from the start. When they discovered that the album was going to be played on what they considered inferior equipment, only Rick Wright actually attended the event.

OPPOSITE: 1972, live onstage in Amsterdam

BELOW: Pink Floyd. L-R: Nick Mason, David Gilmour, Roger Waters and Rick Wright, circa 1973

A couple of months after its release, David Gilmour was still reflecting on how the album was received: "A lot of people, including engineers and roadies, when we asked them, didn't know what the LP was about. I really don't know if our things get through, but you have to carry on hoping." He didn't have much to worry about; press reaction was by and large highly favorable, with Lloyd Grossman being typical of many, enthusing in a *Rolling Stone* review: "There is a certain grandeur here that exceeds mere musical melodramatics and is rarely attempted in rock."

Once again Storm Thorgerson, Aubrey Powell, and the rest of the Hipgnosis team were central to the LP's promotion, with a cover design that proved instantly recognizable, and ultimately memorable. Amid the pomp and pose of early 1970s progressive rock, the gatefold sleeve had come into its own, with increasingly ambitious artwork matching often over-elaborate music. For their new album, Pink Floyd agreed that they should consider a simpler, classier approach. Thorgerson recalled how "Rick Wright suggested we do something clean, elegant and graphic, not photographic." For the project, Hipgnosis worked with their regular collaborator, graphic designer George Hardie, and between them came up with the idea of a glass prism dividing white light into the colors of the spectrum. Hardie created a white line drawing of the prism on a stark black background, with (on Roger Waters' suggestion) the rainbow spectrum of light continuing throughout the gatefold, converting back to white light on the reverse of the sleeve. The design became an instant trademark for what turned out to be one of the most successful albums ever, with the long-player being Pink Floyd's first to top the US charts and elsewhere when it was released, simultaneously hitting the No. 2 spot in the United Kingdom.

And its success was by no means limited to the immediate aftermath of its release. A retrospective review of the album in *Goldmine* magazine in 2008, thirty-five years after its first appearance, uncompromisingly declared: "*Dark Side of the Moon* lives on because, from start to finish and from dawn to dusk, it is a bloody marvelous record, quite possibly the most perfect rock record ever conceived, and undoubtedly the most deserving success story in rock 'n' roll history. And it doesn't matter why." By the early 2020s it had sold over forty-five million copies worldwide, being rated the fourth-biggest-selling album of all time.

OPPOSITE: Roger Waters, Amsterdam, 1972

# The Dark Side of the Moon

Track Listing (original UK vinyl release)

**Side One**
Speak to Me (Nick Mason)
Breathe (In the Air) (Waters, Richard Wright, David
    Gilmour)
On the Run (Gilmour, Waters)
Time (Gilmour, Waters, Wright, Mason)
The Great Gig in the Sky (Wright, Clare Torry [from
    2005])

**Side Two**
Money (Waters)
Us and Them (Waters, Wright)
Any Colour You Like (Gilmour, Mason, Wright)
Brain Damage (Waters)
Eclipse (Waters)

**Recorded:** May 31, 1972 – February 9, 1973, EMI
Studios, London
**Released:** March 10, 1973 (US), March 23, 1973 (UK)
**Label:** Harvest
**Producer:** Pink Floyd
**Personnel:** David Gilmour (guitars, Synthi AKS synthesizer,
vocals), Roger Waters (bass guitar, VCS3
synthesizer, vocals), Richard Wright (keyboards,
VCS3 synthesizer, Synthi AKS synthesizer,
vocals), Nick Mason (drums, percussion)

**Additional Personnel:**
Dick Parry (saxophone), Clare Torry (vocals),
Doris Troy (vocals), Lesley Duncan (vocals),
Liza Strike (vocals), Barry St. John (vocals)

**Chart Position:** UK No. 2, US No. 1, Austria No. 1, Canada
No. 1, Italy No. 1, Australia No. 2, Netherlands
No. 2, Norway No. 2

# wish you were here

"We always like to write numbers, go on the road with them and record them later. We did this with *Dark Side of the Moon*, and we think it's easily the best way to go about it. A number changes so much when we do it live over a long period."

**Rick Wright**

---

OPPOSITE: Pink Floyd in concert at Wembley Arena, London, 1973

ABOVE: Pink Floyd perform live onstage at Merriweather Post Pavilion, Columbia, Maryland, US, 1973

## Touring the Dark Side

When *The Dark Side of the Moon* was released in the US on March 10, 1973, Pink Floyd were already a week into a sixteen-date tour of the United States and Canada. Their set list consisted of the entire album, plus "Obscured by Clouds," "When You're In," and "Careful with That Axe, Eugene," with "One of These Days" as an encore. The line-up was augmented by saxophonist Dick Parry, who had appeared on the album, and backing vocalists Nawasa Crowder, and sisters Phyllis and Mary Ann Lindsey—the trio also known in their own right as the soul group Black Grass. And through the latter half of June, still with the album as the centerpiece, Black Grass (without Nawasa Crowder) appeared on Pink Floyd's second US tour of the year. During the trek, the band set a new record gross by making $110,565 for a single performance, at the Roosevelt Stadium in New Jersey.

Between the US visits, in May the band played two special concerts at London's Earls Court Exhibition Hall in May, in aid of the Shelter National Campaign for the Homeless charity. On this occasion, with Dick Parry still on sax, the backing vocals were provided by the UK singers Vicki Brown and Lisa Strike. Later in the year, at two October concerts in Germany and Austria, Pink Floyd's

vocal accompanists were The Blackberries, featuring seasoned American session singers Billie Barnum, Venetta Fields, and Clydie King. And at a November benefit gig for the Soft Machine drummer Robert Wyatt—who had been rendered disabled after a tragic accident—singers Vicki Brown and Lisa Strike were joined at the London concert by Clare Torry, whose vocalizing on "The Great Gig in the Sky" was one of the highlights of *The Dark Side of the Moon*.

The addition of backing singers and a saxophone to the line-up was symptomatic of the increasingly spectacular and orchestrated stage show that Pink Floyd was presenting by the time of *The Dark Side of the Moon*. It had been a giant leap from the modest light shows they pioneered when the band were ushering in the psychedelic era in the late 1960s, to the highly charged technical extravaganza that now constituted their live appearances all around the world. As two fans at the Earls Court shows of May '73 graphically recorded, the spectacle was indeed unprecedented, with burning gongs, an animated spaceman, the

"inevitable smoke bombs" and dry ice, concluding with "rockets being fired into the roof of the hall, and the tolling of the iron bell, and the knowledge that we had been fortunate, nay privileged, to witness this evening."

A distinct feeling of ennui had set in around the band when it came to their next foray into the recording studio. It seemed as if, when not actually on the road, they were collectively putting off the inevitable—the need for some creative decision-making regarding a new album. One such delaying tactic presented itself in October 1973, when Pink Floyd booked Abbey Road for three weeks, embarking on what became known as the "Household Objects" project. The group were actually reviving a concept they had already experimented with back in 1971, during the recording sessions that eventually produced "Echoes," featured on the *Meddle* album.

The basic idea of the project, with the assistance of studio engineer Alan Parsons, was to create recordings consisting entirely of sounds that were not made by actual musical instruments. The notion obviously appealed to the band's long-time flirtations with concepts considered avant-garde, and as Nick Mason would later admit was a perfect excuse to postpone serious work on a forthcoming album. All manner of domestic sounds were recorded, ranging from the twanging of elastic bands to the slamming of hammers on wood, the tinkle of wine glasses, and the gentle buzz of adhesive tape being unrolled. The group went to great lengths to delay the unavoidable conclusion that the project was getting nowhere—sending roadies on exhaustive shopping trips for household items for instance—but after their twenty days of studio time had elapsed, the scheme was wound up once and for all.

As if to signal some impatience on their part, with no new "product" from the band seemingly likely in the near future, in January 1974, EMI Records—as they had with *Relics* when waiting for *Meddle* to materialize in 1971—released a double LP package entitled *A Nice Pair*. The reissue consisted of Pink Floyd's first two albums, *The Piper at the Gates of Dawn* and *A*

OPPOSITE: Kate Bush pictured in 1978. Bush recorded her first professional demos at David Gilmour's home studio.

ABOVE: Album sleeve (top) and interior (bottom) of Pink Floyd's compilation album, *A Nice Pair*, 1973

*Saucerful of Secrets*, and did moderately well for such a release, making No. 21 and No. 36 in the UK and US charts respectively.

The band themselves, meanwhile, were enjoying life as the true superstars they had become, whether they cared to admit it or not. Rick Wright had purchased a country mansion near Cambridge, in which he set up his own recording studio, The Old Rectory. Nick Mason and his wife Lindy, on the other hand, stayed in central London, buying a town house in Highgate just a few miles north of their

previous abode in Camden. And over the next couple of years, all four lavished their wealth on exotic properties: Nick Mason bought a house in the South of France, Roger Waters chose a villa on the Greek coast, and both Gilmour and Wright acquired villas on the island of Rhodes.

And while Roger Waters had no children with his then-wife Judith, and Gilmour remained unmarried until 1975, by this time there were the natural distractions of growing families. In the case of Rick and his wife Juliette there were two children, Gala and Jamie, while Nick Mason and Lindy were now also parents, with two-year-old Chloe.

Although the group seemed in no hurry to get down to some serious work vis-à-vis the next Pink Floyd long-player, various musical collaborations attracted individual attentions. Nick had got himself involved with the folk rock and performance art group Principal Edwards (formerly Principal Edwards Magic Theatre), producing their album *Round One*. Nick was also involved with Soft Machine's Robert Wyatt, before and in the aftermath of the debilitating accident which had left Wyatt

wheelchair-bound. He produced Wyatt's album *Rock Bottom*, released in July 1974, and an unexpected version of the Monkees' "I'm a Believer," which hit the charts at No. 29 and led to a return appearance for Mason on BBC TV's *Top of the Pops*.

During Pink Floyd's voluntary furlough, David Gilmour was also busying himself in various directions. As well as gigging occasionally with the Scottish folk rock outfit Sutherland Brothers and Quiver, Gilmour went on to produce the debut album of country rock band Unicorn, *Blue Pine Trees*, after first hearing them at a wedding party. Unicorn achieved some modest level of success, primarily in America, and David went on to produce their next three albums over the following four years or so. And it was via Unicorn that David became aware of a young singer-songwriter by the name of Kate Bush, who recorded her first demos at his home studio.

But clearly, if Pink Floyd were to still have a future as an active, creative unit, they couldn't just sit on their hands for ever. As David Gilmour reflected, it was time for the band to assess where they stood in the grand scheme of things: "You hit that

strange impasse where you're really not certain of anything anymore . . . what on earth do we do now?"

In an effort to break the stalemate they seemed to have found themselves in, on June 18, 1974, the band embarked on a short, seven-date French tour, beginning in Toulouse and finishing off with three dates at the Palais des Sports in Paris. The concerts were of significance in that the band, as well as performing their now-usual *Dark Side of the Moon* in its entirety, debuted what would be the major work on their next album, "Shine On You Crazy Diamond," plus "Raving and Drooling," which eventually appeared as "Sheep" on 1977's *Animals*. And the French gigs also marked Pink Floyd's first use of a

**"You hit that strange impasse where you're really not certain of anything anymore . . . what on earth do we do now?"**

**David Gilmour**

tour was titled "The Pink Floyd: Super All-Action Official Music Programme for Boys and Girls," designed in the style of a kids' comic, with a portrait of the band by the celebrated cartoonist Gerald Scarfe. The booklet included comic strips of the group as their alter egos—"Rog of the Rovers," "Captain Mason RN," "Dave Derring," and "Rich Right."

Interviewed for *Melody Maker* during the UK tour, Rick Wright confirmed that the new numbers were probably destined to appear on a future album (or albums), whenever that might occur: "We always like to write numbers, go on the road with them and record them later. We did this with *Dark Side of the Moon*, and we think it's easily the best way to go about it. A number changes so much when we do it live over a long period; 'Shine On' has changed a lot since we started already."

## Studio Time

The band's next album began to become a reality from January 13, 1975, when they booked studio time at Abbey Road that would continue intermittently until the beginning of March. After a short North American tour through April, the band reconvened for recording in May, then again (following another transatlantic visit) in early July. Predictably, after their extended lay-off from the studio, the renewed discipline and concentration required for recording didn't come instantly. Nick Mason, for one, was distracted by the trauma of a disintegrating marriage, and early sessions were often plagued by tardiness or absence, with the band sometimes spending more time drinking and playing darts than laying down sounds. But gradually things began to come together satisfactorily with "Shine On You Crazy Diamond," and the other two road-tested songs.

Roger Waters made it clear very early on in the process that "Shine On You Crazy Diamond," which would be the key composition on the new album, was closely related to his affectionate reflections on the band's old comrade Syd Barrett. With that in mind, the overall theme of the collection was, according to Waters, one of "absence." And as a consequence, neither of the other two new songs the band had been trying out onstage made it to the immediate track list in hand. The music

huge circular projection screen, which became a trademark of the band's live performances from there on.

So, during the second half of 1974, the band slowly began coming together again in terms of some new material. As well as the two numbers introduced in France, another fresh song— "You've Got to Be Crazy"—appeared on the set list when they made their only other live appearances during 1974, on a short twenty-date UK tour in November and December. The number, like "Raving and Drooling," would be released on *Animals*, in this case renamed as "Dogs." The souvenir program for the British

that did appear on Pink Floyd's next album, however, would be subsequently hailed as one of the band's landmark achievements.

Beginning with what one writer would describe as "the most famous four notes in Pink Floyd's history," Gilmour's opening guitar solo on the first part of "Shine On You Crazy Diamond" follows a four-minute intro embellished by Rick Wright's inspired flourishes on synthesizer and organ; plus a remnant from the "Household Objects" sessions, a musical tone created by rubbing the rim of a wine glass. The impact of the soaring guitar is one of sonic grandeur, and a good eight minutes transpire before any vocals are heard on the track. Waters comes in with the lyrics, addressed directly to his memories of Barrett, rich in texture and supported by the backing voices of Venetta Fields and Carlena Williams. The instrumental passages that follow feature saxophone man Dick Parry in full flight, first in the meatier lower registers of the baritone sax, then on his more usual tenor horn. There was more to come of "Shine On . . ." later in the album, as the subtitle of the thirteen-minute track, "Parts I–V," hinted.

Why Roger Waters (and, as with most major decisions made at that time, it *was* solely down to Waters) decided to sandwich the magnum opus either side of three seemingly unrelated tracks has always been open to debate. One view was that it retained the "concept" feel of the album as a whole, rather than having one side consisting purely of "Shine On . . ." and Waters' other songs relegated to a secondary place in the running order.

Whatever, "Parts VI–IX" is a much more understated listening experience. Again, Waters' lyrics—minimal at just eight lines—directly address the band's erstwhile founder member, at this time still revered by many long-term Floyd fans as embodying the now-lost essence of their music. Much of the laid-back ride-out to the album might have come as something of an anti-climax, compared to the passion of the first section of the piece.

Rich in layer upon layer of Rick Wright's synth effects, "Welcome to the Machine," which followed the initial rendering of "Shine On . . ." on the vinyl release, evokes a sinister, dystopian world in

which we are all at the mercy of forces beyond our control. A chilling analogy to the Kafkaesque workings of the music business, a subject close to Waters' heart, it can also be read as an even more focused nod in the direction of Syd Barrett's sad experience as a rock 'n' roll casualty.

Waters' other direct critique of the record industry came in "Have a Cigar." According to in-studio accounts, Roger's singing voice was almost out of action after constant re-takes of "Shine On . . ." and David Gilmour—unhappy about the unabashed politics of the lyrics—was reluctant to step in as vocalist. Coincidentally, an old friend of the band, the singer-songwriter Roy Harper, was working in the studio next door on his new album *HQ*. A strident radical in his own songs, Harper was at one with Roger's take on showbiz machinations, and happy to voice the latter's acerbic lyrics. The hard-edged delivery from Harper complements a tough-sounding, straight-ahead rock backing, hardly typical of Floyd in its simplicity.

Befitting the title track of the album, "Wish You Were Here" is as straightforward a song as you are likely to hear on any Pink Floyd collection. An interesting footnote to the recording of the number was the presence of the eminent jazz violinist Stéphane Grappelli. The French virtuoso was working in a

ABOVE: Pink Floyd play football in France following their concert in Dijon on June 21, 1974

OPPOSITE: Onstage at Earls Court as part of a benefit gig for homeless charity, Shelter, May 1973

LEFT: The program for two Pink Floyd concerts at Earls Court, London, 1973

neighboring studio at Abbey Road with his classical counterpart Yehudi Menuhin, and David Gilmour suggested he sit in on a final coda to the track. In the event, his contribution was hardly audible in the final mix. Again, the references to Syd Barrett are hardly veiled in the lyrics, and David Gilmour's vocals, supported by his acoustic twelve-string guitar, make the chorus refrain particularly poignant.

## Syd

Thoughts about Syd Barrett suddenly took on a whole new focus on June 5, 1975, when the singer turned up at one of the recording sessions, totally unannounced and unexpected. The band were about to take off for their next American tour,

commencing June 7, and they were finishing the mix of "Shine On You Crazy Diamond" when the former front man arrived to everyone's amazement. At first, some there, including Roger Waters and Nick Mason, didn't recognize their old comrade. Barrett had gained much weight, had a shaven head, and looked generally unkempt and disheveled. Gilmour, who initially thought he was a studio staff member, was the first to realize the stranger's identity, and the others reacted with shock and disbelief when it became clear who it was.

In his memoir, Mason described how he was "horrified by the physical change" of the musician who had been a central catalyst in the birth and early glories of Pink Floyd. It transpired that Barrett had turned up to attend David Gilmour's wedding reception, which was being held in the adjoining EMI canteen,

the guitarist having married his first wife, the American artist Virginia "Ginger" Hasenbein, earlier that day. After some casual comments about the recording that was being played back, Syd disappeared as surreptitiously as he had made his entrance. Storm Thorgerson recalled the incident, and its impact on those there at the time: "Two or three people cried. He sat round and talked for a bit, but he wasn't really there." Apart from Roger Waters apparently coming across him by chance in a London department store a year or two later, it would be the last time any of the band would come face to face with their former bandmate.

Following his departure from Pink Floyd in 1968, Syd Barrett's career had been in decline. At first enthusiastically nurtured by ex-Floyd managers Pete Jenner and Andrew King, after a year out of the public eye, in January 1970, Syd released the first of two solo albums, *The Madcap Laughs*. His ex-colleagues in Pink Floyd were still very much supportive of Barrett, to the degree that both Waters and Gilmour assisted on the album in a production capacity, with Gilmour also appearing on guitars throughout. Although work on the recordings had begun soon after Syd's departure from the Floyd, the bulk of the album was recorded between April and July 1969, with five producers credited—Barrett, Peter Jenner, Malcom Jones, plus Waters and

Gilmour.

In the event, the album was a moderate success, reaching No. 40 in the UK chart, and garnered some positive responses in the music press. Talking to Syd after the release, Chris Welch of *Melody Maker*—who described the album as a "strained, halting, but often beautiful set of songs"—asked whether he was satisfied with the LP. The singer's reply was typically enigmatic: "Well, no. I always find recording difficult. I can only think in terms of, well I'm pleased with forty minutes of sound, but I can't in terms of the pop industry. It's only a beginning—I've written a lot more stuff." Commenting on the release, Roger Waters declared: "Syd is a genius."

Syd began recording his second solo release in February 1970, while *The Madcap Laughs* was still hot in the shops. Sessions for the eponymously titled *Barrett* were sporadic, lasting until July, and featured Dave Gilmour and Rick Wright as both instrumentalists and producers. Unlike its predecessor, the album failed to make even a modest showing on the charts. Rick Wright would recall how difficult it had been, sometimes even to get Barrett focused on the job in hand: "By then it was just trying to help Syd any way we could . . . It was just going into the studio, and trying to get him to sing."

From then on, Syd's professional life became increasingly hit-and-miss. His lifestyle was more and more reclusive, although in 1974 Pete Jenner managed to persuade him to return to Abbey Road with a view to making another record. He recorded eleven tracks in all, but none were released, after which he left the music industry altogether. It came as even more of a serendipitous surprise, therefore, when he suddenly appeared at the Pink Floyd session in July '75, just as the band were finalizing Roger Waters' heartfelt paean to their former comrade and inspiration.

## Release

A week after concluding their second North American tour of 1975, on July 5, Pink Floyd played their one and only gig in the UK that year, a major outdoor event staged at Knebworth Park, in Hertfordshire. The band headlined a bill that also featured The Steve Miller Band, Captain Beefheart and his Magic Band, their recent guest vocalist Roy Harper with his group Trigger, and singer Linda Lewis.

The long-awaited appearance began with the new songs from their forthcoming album. Naturally, the fresh material was unfamiliar to most of the crowd, unlike the complete *Dark Side of the Moon* which followed in their second set. But as the reviewer from *Sounds* enthused, the sheer sonic experience of a Pink Floyd concert made an immediate impression beyond the impact of the music itself: "Floyd have the ingenuity and skill to spring from a deceptively simple melodic base into the most esoteric of electronic realms, using the quadrophonic speaker system as a series of walls off which notes are bounced and skimmed around the arena, at one moment with a ruthless metallic compulsion, at another with the mystic, transcendental intensity of North African holy music."

Two months later, a full eighteen months after the release of *Dark Side of the Moon*, Pink Floyd released their ninth studio album, *Wish You Were Here*. Again created by the team at Hipgnosis, the packaging—which went far beyond the confines of a simple cover—was even more ambitious than the sleeve concept that became the trademark for the previous album. To the consternation of the record companies on both sides of the Atlantic, Thorgerson and the band proposed to surround the cover with black shrink-wrap, therefore making the sleeve art "absent" in keeping with the general theme of the music. Despite both Harvest in the UK and Columbia in the US opposing the idea, the band overruled their objections, and the concept went ahead.

Illustrator George Hardie—the key collaborator on the *Dark Side of the Moon* packaging—provided an image of two mechanical hands in a handshake, which was attached to the black wrap-around as a sticker. The image would also be used on the disc's actual label. "There's nothing better at Christmas than you get a present that's wrapped up and you tear off the wrapping paper, you look inside, and then the box, and you open the box and there's your present," Thorgerson's partner at Hipgnosis, Aubrey "Po" Powell, would explain. "Well, the same thing applied when we did *Wish You Were Here*."

The key image on the front cover was photographed by Powell. It involved what appeared to be two businessmen, shaking hands as if clinching a deal, but with one of the pair on fire. The controversial picture was inspired by the idea that true feelings are covered up in financial dealings, and—especially pertinent to the music business—people often "get burned" in the process. The photography took place

OPPOSITE: Pink Floyd concert poster, 1975

FROM ENGLAND
PINK FLOYD
INITIAL SHOCK
A.B. SKHY BLUES BAND
JERRY ABRAMS HEADLIGHTS
SOUND FACTORY
AUGUST 16·17
1217 ALHAMBRA 9·1
$3.00 SACRAMENTO
TICKET OUTLETS: Sacramento - All Tower locations, Jack's House of Music, The Tape Shop, Village Records, Bruener's Box Office, The Eye, All College Hi Shops; Davis - U.C. Corner; Woodland - Bender's Music; Marysville - Sievwright's Music; Stockton - Weberstown Box Office, Miracle Music; Roseville - Roseville Records, Roseville Music.
PARK UNDER THE FREEWAY AT 19TH & L STREETS

in the Warner Bros. film studios in the Los Angeles suburb of Burbank. Two Hollywood stuntmen were employed on the shoot, with one wearing fireproof clothing under his "business suit." The painstaking process was testament to Thorgerson's work ethic that all Hipgnosis imagery was "real," rather than photographs being manipulated afterwards. As Dave Gilmour conceded years later, "I still think it's an excellent sleeve. With computer packages like Photoshop you could produce a sleeve like that a lot more easily these days, but somehow I don't think it would be the same. I think it's a great cover."

The back cover illustration was equally enigmatic, with a faceless and limbless "salesman" figure displaying his wares—the Floyd vinyl album inside the sleeve—again photographed by Powell, in the Yuma Desert in Arizona. Powell's pictures for the inner sleeve, a "splashless" shot of a diver taken at Mono Lake in California, and a red veil concealing a nude model, wafting in the breeze taken in a grove of trees in Norfolk, England, retained the surreal ambience of all the images surrounding the album.

Despite receiving some mixed reviews, *Wish You Were Here* shot to the top of the UK charts the week after its release on September 12. It simultaneously hit the No. 1 spot in America, the band's first release on the Columbia label. Manager Steve O'Rourke had not been happy with the performance of Capitol (EMI's label for US releases) regarding Pink Floyd, and secured a deal with Columbia, while the band continued on EMI's Harvest label in the UK and Europe. On its release, the album also topped the chart in at least half a dozen other countries worldwide.

Contrasting with the album's immediate success with the record-buying public, many critics greeted it with less than universal acclaim, although there were plenty of positive reviews. In *Let It Rock* magazine, Mick Gold concluded: "This may not be Pink Floyd's most inspired record, but it confirms them as a great band: a perplexing blend of professional brilliance and low-key personalities." *Melody Maker*, on the other hand, disparagingly spoke of the album's "bleak, emotionally barren landscapes," and another scribe described it as "well crafted, pleasant, and utterly without challenge, it's mood music for a new age." Since then the album's status has risen exponentially over the years, it being cited many times as one of the greatest rock albums of all time. In retrospect both Dave Gilmour and Rick Wright named it as their favorite album by the band, despite the sometimes fractious recording process that would have an impact on the band during the coming years.

OPPOSITE: Roger Waters performing live onstage with Pink Floyd at the Nassau Coliseum, Long Island, New York, June 16, 1975

# Wish You Were Here

Track Listing (original UK vinyl release)

### Side One
Shine On You Crazy Diamond (Parts I–V) (Roger
    Waters, David Gilmour, Richard Wright)
Welcome to the Machine (Waters)

### Side Two
Have a Cigar (Waters)
Wish You Were Here (Waters, Gilmour)
Shine On You Crazy Diamond (Parts VI–IX)
    (Wright, Gilmour, Waters—Parts VI–VIII),
    (Wright—Part IX)

| | |
|---|---|
| **Recorded:** | January 13 – July 28, 1975, EMI Studios, London |
| **Released:** | September 12, 1975 (UK), September 13, 1975 (US) |
| **Label:** | Harvest (UK), Columbia (US) |
| **Producer:** | Pink Floyd |
| **Personnel:** | David Gilmour (guitars, Synthi AKS synthesizer, bass, harmonica, vocals), Roger Waters (bass guitar, VCS3 synthesizer, guitar, harmonica, vocals), Richard Wright (keyboards, VCS3 synthesizer, Hammond organ, vocals), Nick Mason (drums, percussion) |
| **Additional Personnel:** | |
| | Dick Parry (saxophones), Roy Harper (vocals), Venetta Fields (vocals), Carlena Williams (vocals), Stéphane Grappelli (violin) |
| **Chart Position:** | UK No. 1, US No. 1, Australia No. 1, Finland No. 1, Netherlands No. 1, Italy No. 1, New Zealand No. 1, Spain No. 1, Austria No. 2, Norway No. 2 |

# animals

"There was one guy in the front row shouting and screaming all the way through . . . I called him over and, when he got close enough, spat in his face."

Roger Waters

## Britannia Row

**F**ollowing *Wish You Were Here*, Pink Floyd took what amounted to a lengthy sabbatical from touring, but were nevertheless relatively productive during the subsequent seventeen months off the road.

During the making of the previous album, various schisms within the band had become more apparent. These were mainly surrounding Roger Waters' increasingly dominant role as the key conceptual driver of the band's material, despite the crucial musical contribution of the other three, particularly David Gilmour and Rick Wright. Some of these fissures were evident on the group's tour dates over a year or so before the lay-off, when Storm Thorgerson and Roger Waters' friend Nick Sedgwick accompanied the band, with a view to putting together a "definitive" account of Pink Floyd on the road. As it transpired the book was never published—partly resulting from pressure from Gilmour—but as Thorgerson would recall, "It does display the dynamic in the group at that time. I had tapes of certain discussions, some arguments. At times, perhaps people said things they wished they hadn't."

Whatever the underlying tensions surrounding Pink Floyd on a creative level,

Roger Waters (above) and David Gilmour (opposite) live onstage with Pink Floyd, Wembley Empire Pool, London, March, 1977

from a purely business perspective they seemed to be singing from the same songbook when as a group they purchased an old three-storey block of church buildings at 35 Britannia Row, in the north London borough of Islington. The plan was to convert the premises to a recording studio facility—much in the spirit of The Kinks with their Konk Studios, and The Who's Pete Townshend with Eel Pie—along with warehouse space for the group's vast array of stage equipment, and a top floor that would serve as offices for the band. The studio would also be hired out to other bands and artists.

And there was a logic to the arrangement from a financial point of view. Pink Floyd's deal with EMI Records included them taking a cut in their sales percentage in exchange for unlimited studio time at Abbey Road—hence the inordinate length of sessions devoted to certain tracks—but that agreement had now expired. It was therefore a money-saver, they figured, to own their own facility which they could also rent to others when they were not using it. And there was the added bonus of hiring out their stage equipment when they were not on tour, but in the event few bands required the lavish quadraphonic sound effects and lighting associated

with the Floyd, and that aspect of their business model soon proved a non-starter.

Nevertheless, Britannia Row was up and running as a new recording venue for the band when they began working on their next album in April 1976, which would mark the almost complete domination of the composition side of things by Roger Waters. On *Wish You Were Here*, Waters' writing credits were shared by other members of the band on three of the five tracks, while on the new LP four of the five numbers would be assigned solely to the bass player. Waters likewise sang lead vocals on every track, bar one he shared with Gilmour, with his assumed leadership becoming a bone of contention that would get worse—and sometimes explode acrimoniously—throughout the eight months of recording at Britannia Row. While the tension was most obvious between David Gilmour and Roger Waters, Rick Wright too felt increasingly marginalized in favor of Waters' relentless takeover of the band. As he would comment about the album in a TV documentary some years later: "I didn't contribute to the writing of it, but I think that also Roger was kind of not letting me do that. That was the start of the whole ego thing in the band."

> ## "I didn't contribute to the writing of it, but I think that also Roger was kind of not letting me do that. That was the start of the whole ego thing in the band."
>
> ### Rick Wright

OPPOSITE: Rick Wright, Wembley Empire Pool, March 1977

RIGHT: A pop-up cardboard display for the Pink Floyd album *Animals* up for auction at Christie's in London, November 29, 2012. It sold for more than £500.

PAGES 150-151: Pink Floyd perform live onstage at Pavillon de Paris, France, February 22, 1977

PAGES 152-153: Pink Floyd, March 1977, UK *Animals* tour

## Concept

Ego thing or not, Roger Waters' concept for the next album by Pink Floyd was certainly audacious, and (surprisingly, some would say) in keeping with the fractious mood of the times. Mid-seventies Britain was riven with industrial and social unrest, and the millionaire lifestyles of rock stars like Pink Floyd seemed at odds with the situation that most young people found themselves in. Many younger music fans felt increasingly alienated by the posing and pretensions of so-called "progressive" rock stars—Floyd, Yes, Genesis, and the rest—as British punk music raised its spiky head in the latter half of 1976.

The raw grass-roots music emanating from the pub rock circuit and newly established punk clubs, with its short-sharp-shock songs played at a furious pace, was in stark contrast to the increasingly remote posturing that groups like the Floyd had come to exemplify. In the hands of bands like The Damned and The Clash, it was often music with a social message and a rebellious attitude to go with it. And ironically, despite the Floyd's ambitious stage presentation and state-of-the-art recordings, it had much in common with the sociopolitical stance that Roger Waters had continually adopted in much of his songwriting.

Plus of course, there was a shared healthy skepticism about the music business establishment, which Waters had promoted since the band's early days as psychedelic rebels at UFO.

Nevertheless, Pink Floyd were universally regarded by the new wave of musicians—plus their noisy supporters in the music press—as part of the old guard of rock 'n' roll dinosaurs, about to be swept away on a tidal wave of musical change. As Nick Mason reflected: "The punk movement was the moment when we found ourselves on the wrong end of a cultural revolution, just as we had been very much on the right end of it during the underground days of 1966 and 1967."

A number of accounts over the years have suggested that Roger Waters' concept for the new album was directly inspired by George Orwell's 1945 book *Animal Farm*. In that novel, the animals take over the farmyard, only to be overruled in turn by the dictatorial pigs—the target of the critique being the Stalinism that had been born out of ideological communism in the Soviet Union. But Waters' criticism was actually aimed far nearer home, at contemporary capitalism, with new material created against the backdrop of the punk upheaval going on in the world of popular music.

The initially unrelated songs were developed by Roger into a thematic commentary on modern society and its moral shortcomings, drawing parallels with the state of humanity and that of animals. Through the latter half of 1976 Waters brought together his vision of a dystopian future in which the human race was replaced by three species of animals—dogs, pigs, and sheep. The animals were a metaphor for human characteristics: the aggressive, violent dogs, the dictatorial pigs, and the acquiescent, unthinking sheep. As Roger explained in a six-part radio documentary at the time of the album's release: "Sometime during the middle of recording, it seemed like the right thing to tie it all together . . . I've had the idea of *Animals* in the back of my mind for years . . . many years." Two of the numbers, "Sheep" and "Dogs," were actually modifications, of "Raving and Drooling" and "You've Got to Be Crazy" respectively, both of which had been debuted onstage during Pink Floyd's brief tours of France and the UK in 1974.

## The Album

The final running order of the release was something of a contrivance on Roger Waters' part, with the light, acoustic opener "Pigs on the Wing"—a lyrical tribute to his newlywed wife Carolyne—split into two short segments of just one verse each, opening and closing the album. He'd written the song some time before the first *Animals* sessions at Britannia Row, and the decision to split it in this way almost suggests he was anxious to add some optimism to the otherwise doom-laden flavor of the collection. A more jaundiced view, not lost on the rest of the band, implied that bookending the number assured Waters of two, rather than one, track-by-track royalties. It would be one of several bones of contention regarding the financial disbursements from the album.

The delicate touch of the opening song rendered the follow-up, "Dogs," as even more of a shock to the system. With its no-holds-barred dynamics redolent of the fast-and-furious punk music taking the music world by storm, despite its lengthy seventeen minutes it maintained the latter's angst and fury in Waters' acerbic lyrics. It was the only track not credited to Roger Waters alone, with David Gilmour rightly sharing recognition in what was a tour de force on the part of the guitarist. Not to mention Gilmour's vocals, which alternated with Waters' to paint a picture of a doomed money-man reaping his just desserts. Writing-wise, Gilmour's contribution to the album as a whole was understandably restricted by the distraction of his wife Ginger having their first child. And both Rick Wright and Nick Mason supplied far less than usual to the compositions, with it being the first album by the band not to include any writing credit to Wright.

The second side of the vinyl release opened with "Pigs (Three Different Ones)," with a verse each dedicated to three contemporary targets of Roger Waters' ire. Even now, well into the twenty-first century, the sheer violence of the song's delivery reflects the bass player's anger: first addressed to a typical "fat cat" capitalist, then to the leader of the UK Conservative Party (and later Prime Minister) Margaret Thatcher, and thirdly the puritanical campaigner for old-fashioned "moral values" in the British media, Mary Whitehouse.

In "Sheep," Waters uses the ruminant characters in his parable on modern life, to exemplify the struggle between the weakest and strongest. Perhaps most controversially, he takes the revered Psalm 23 ("The Lord is my shepherd") from the Bible as a basis for his spoken-word "sermon." The passive fate of slaughtered sheep for slaughter—". . . he converteth me to lamb cutlets"—is followed by the sheep's dramatic volte-face, when they lethally turn on the dogs who are attacking them. Instrumentally, it's classic Floyd, with Rick's understated, bluesy piano (backed with some hillside bleating of lambs) launching into the rocking main theme. The "sermon" interlude comes after six minutes or so, with a knocked-back voice distorted almost beyond recognition, before the tempo reasserts itself into a triumphal ride-out—accompanied, once again, by sheep in their countryside idyll.

OPPOSITE: Nick Mason performing live onstage, New Bingley Hall, Stafford, UK, 1977

ABOVE: An inflatable pig floats above the stage as Pink Floyd perform in Goffertpark, Netherlands

## Pigs Might Fly

By this time generally considered—even by the rest of the group—as Pink Floyd's de facto ideas man-in-chief, it was perhaps inevitable that Roger Waters would be the creative source behind the band's new album art. Hipgnosis, as unofficial "house" design team for the Floyd, were approached for some ideas for *Animals*, but in the event the core idea for the sleeve illustration came from the bass player.

It was late in 1976, with the studio work on *Animals* completed, that the band began considering the cover. They were not convinced by the three suggestions put forward by Hipgnosis, when Roger came up with an idea that stuck. At the time he was living in Clapham, just south of the River Thames in London, so almost every day he was driving up to the Britannia Row studios in Islington, passing the iconic Battersea Power Station on the way. The skyline landmark, with its four soaring chimneys, had originated in the 1930s, and was completed in its present form in the 1950s. By the 1970s it was already on the way to industrial redundancy, and would close completely in 1983, when it was designated and preserved as a Grade II listed building, on account of its unique art deco design.

Roger proposed having a giant inflatable pig—reflecting the optimism of "Pigs on the Wing"—to be photographed suspended from the four towers, appearing as if flying across the building. Storm Thorgerson and his team agreed to help stage the photoshoot, and the band commissioned a 30-foot helium balloon, to be created by the German company Ballon Fabrik, creators of the original Zeppelins in World War I. On December 2, the giant pig was assembled and inflated at the power station, with a team of fourteen photographers at the ready. As a precaution a professional marksman was on hand, just in case the tethering between the towers failed, and the creature—which the band had dubbed "Algie"—floated away.

The weather, however, took a turn for the worse, and the shoot was postponed until the next day. All went well on the second attempt, with Algie guided up between the chimneys, until a gust of wind tore the pig from its mooring ropes. Unfortunately, manager Steve O'Rourke had omitted to re-hire the marksman for the second day, and the colossal porker went sailing into the blue beyond. Chaos ensued, with reports of astonished airline pilots spotting the pig, and flights cancelled by air traffic control at Heathrow Airport. Eventually, the pig landed on some farmland in Kent, with the farmer furious that airborne Algie had apparently scared his cows. Though most of the consequences were unintended, the whole saga of the flying pig came over in the media as a brilliant publicity stunt.

Unfortunately, Algie never appeared on the final album cover. The best shots of the power station, against a moody, cloudy landscape, were taken on some earlier preliminary shoots. So the picture of the pig as seen by the record-buying public was actually

superimposed, rather than one taken at the memorable event itself. And the image of the flying pig, from there on, became something of a trademark for Pink Floyd, often appearing as inflatables at live gigs, and on all manner of tour and publicity paraphernalia.

## Release

Prior to the album release, on December 17, Capital Radio in London launched a major documentary series, *The Pink Floyd Story*, with six weekly forty-five-minute episodes concluding on January 21, 1977, the day *Animals* hit the shops. Described as the most detailed account of the group's history to date, the programs included interviews with every band member, plus studio outtakes and segments from live shows. The key series presenter, DJ Nicky Horne, was somewhat miffed, however, when after promising an exclusive airing of *Animals* in the concluding episode, he was pipped at the post by the BBC's John Peel, who played the album in its entirety on his Radio One show the evening before.

There was a press conference launch for the album staged

at Battersea Power Station (where else?), two days before the release date, with the album being played in full, followed by a question-and-answer session. None of the band turned up for the event, and manager Steve O'Rourke was obliged to field all the comments and queries. It was as if the four principals already anticipated a muted response to their latest release, and in many cases their fears proved well-founded. While *Melody Maker*'s Karl Dallas welcomed the work as an "uncomfortable taste of reality in a medium that has become in recent years, increasingly soporific," and Robert Christgau praised "a piece of well-constructed political program music . . . lyrical, ugly, and rousing, all in the right places" in New York's *Village Voice*, writers like *Rolling Stone*'s Frank Rose described the band as "bitter and morose," concluding: "Space doesn't offer any kind of real escape; Pink Floyd knows that. But spacing out is supposed to. (Spacing out has always been the idea behind space rock anyway.) *Animals* is Floyd's attempt to deal with the realization that spacing out isn't the answer either. There's no exit; you get high, you come down again. That's what Pink Floyd has done, with a thud."

Just two days after the album was released, the band embarked on a promotional tour of Europe, taking in dates in Germany, Austria, Switzerland, the Netherlands, Belgium, and France, ending with nine concerts in England. According to Nick Mason, this was the first time the band went out on the road on a specifically "branded" tour to promote their latest album. Entitled "The In The Flesh Tour" (and also known as the *Animals* tour), it was the most ambitious outing by the band yet, in terms of the sheer spectacle of their stage presentation.

The airborne pig was omnipresent at every performance, floating above the

OPPOSITE: A ticket for a Pink Floyd concert at Wembley Empire Pool, London, March 19, 1977

ABOVE: Radio DJ Nicky Horne (center) who presented a six-part documentary series, *The Pink Floyd Story*, ahead of the release of *Animals* in 1977. Also pictured are Brian James of The Damned (left) and Nick Mason (right).

## "*Animals* is Floyd's attempt to deal with the realization that spacing out isn't the answer either. There's no exit; you get high, you come down again. That's what Pink Floyd has done, with a thud."

### *Rolling Stone*

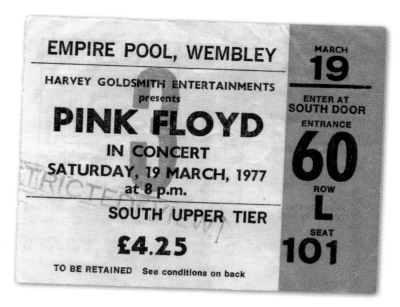

EMPIRE POOL, WEMBLEY

HARVEY GOLDSMITH ENTERTAINMENTS
presents

**PINK FLOYD**

IN CONCERT
SATURDAY, 19 MARCH, 1977
at 8 p.m.

SOUTH UPPER TIER

£4.25

TO BE RETAINED   See conditions on back

MARCH
**19**

ENTER AT
SOUTH DOOR
ENTRANCE

**60**

ROW
**L**

SEAT
**101**

audience before the opening set, and in some cases (a cheaper version) would explode over the crowd. Likewise, at some outdoor venues fireworks were set off that released parachutes shaped as sheep, which floated down over the fans.

Another element in the visual presentation was a film projector operating from a 17-foot tower behind the stage, projecting onto a 32-foot screen suspended at the back of the stage. It featured some startling animations commissioned specifically for the shows, by the eminent cartoonist and illustrator Gerald Scarfe, who had worked with Pink Floyd on a caricature of the group for the center spread of their 1974–75 tour program.

On the North American leg of the tour, which began in late April, the marketing side of things was even more aggressive, with four nights over the Fourth of July weekend at New York's Madison Square Garden, preceded by a Pink Floyd "Parade" on Sixth Avenue that involved inflatable animals at a fan gathering in Central Park. Journalist Barry Miles described the scene in the *New Musical Express*, as the pig motif was introduced: "The Floyd filled the place with smoke and brought out a huge inflatable pig—like the Goodyear blimp—which cruised about the vast space of the auditorium, the pencil beams of light from its eyes casting a malevolent gaze over the stalls. It came to rest and hovered, as if about to take a dump on the mixing console. For a while, several thousand people couldn't see the group because there was a huge pig in the way."

On account of the extravagant visual effects—mostly not directly related to the music, it has to be said—tour venues were restricted to larger auditoriums and stadiums. Onstage, the band itself was augmented by just two supporting musicians, their now-familiar sax player Dick Parry, and a new addition, guitarist Terence "Snowy" White.

An old friend of Fleetwood Mac founder Peter Green, White had been invited to Britannia Row to discuss the gig prior to

the tour, but when he got there he found the atmosphere in the studio was "terrible." It transpired that he'd arrived just after a key solo by Dave Gilmour had been accidentally erased, hence the pervading tension. "Dave took me to the office and told me what the gig was all about, and asked me if I fancied doing it," White recalled. "I said 'Can we have a bit of a play or jam or something,' and he said 'Well you wouldn't be here if you couldn't play would you?' So with that curt reply, he was hired. Before White left the studio, however, Roger Waters suggested he play something, and an impromptu solo by the guitarist was recorded, and used on *Animals* as a link between the two sections of "Pigs on the Wing." Snowy's contribution, however, only found its way onto the 8-track cartridge release of the album. On the tour itself, White helped kick things off by playing bass guitar on "Sheep," then fluctuating between bass and rhythm guitars throughout the sets, and soloing as lead guitar on "Have a Cigar." And his presence in the band did seem to inspire David Gilmour (who was otherwise not at his happiest during the trek), most memorably when the pair traded some dynamic guitar licks on "Shine On You Crazy Diamond."

But notwithstanding moments of musical inspiration, the tour was a mixed blessing for all concerned. Dave Gilmour was already at odds with Waters over the distribution of songwriting royalties for *Animals*, especially when Waters split his three-minute "Pigs on the Wing" to begin and end the album, therefore earning three times the royalties that Gilmour did for his major co-contribution to the seventeen-minute "Dogs." During the tour there were more immediate sources of tension between the guitarist and bass player, not least bad feeling between their respective partners. Dave's wife Ginger, who came on the tour with their baby Alice, certainly didn't see eye to eye with Roger's new "posh" wife Carolyne Christie. By the end of the tour Gilmour was more than despondent

about his place in the band, which he felt had now reached the pinnacle of success, with nowhere further to go.

Rick Wright too, was on the verge of saying goodbye to Pink Floyd as the tour progressed. He had been concerned for some time that the band's music was being overwhelmed by their technical gadgetry, both in the studio and onstage. This came to a head during the tour. At a concert in Frankfurt, Germany, a near-riot broke out when irate fans could hardly see the band for the large amount of dry ice being used, and on many occasions the sheer size of the eighty-thousand-seater stadiums literally dwarfed what was actually happening onstage. Things became so fraught on the road, that at one stage Wright flew back to England from the US, threatening to leave the band there and then.

And for Roger Waters, who now often arrived and departed from venues separately from the rest of the band, things seemingly reached breaking point on the very last night of the tour. The concert was in Montreal, Canada, and a particularly rowdy crowd tested the bass player's patience to the limit. "There was one guy in the front row shouting and screaming all the way through," Waters would recall. "I called him over and, when he got close enough, spat in his face." He would admit he shocked himself by his reaction, realizing immediately this wasn't the way things were meant to be.

Whatever the crises and personal dramas that dogged the tour, as a live promotion for *Animals*, plus the attendant publicity, it certainly paid off. The album reached the No. 2 spot in the UK and No. 3 in the United States, as well as topping the charts in five other territories around the globe. But the band as a unit entered a period of creative hiatus, as both Dave Gilmour and Rick Wright recorded and released their first solo albums; Nick Mason, meanwhile, got involved in the production of the Steve Hillage album *Green*.

It was now dependent, even more so than before, on Roger Waters to come up with ideas for the next album by Pink Floyd, which wouldn't see the light of day until nearly two years after the release of *Animals*. Ironically, a key seed of those ideas was sown on that last night in Montreal, when Waters sensed that an unintended division, albeit of their own making, had developed between the band and their audiences.

OPPOSITE: David Gilmour plays guitar live onstage during Pink Floyd's four-night run at Madison Square Garden, New York, July 1977

# Animals

Track Listing (original UK vinyl release)

### Side One
Pigs on the Wing (Part One) (Roger Waters)
Dogs (Waters, David Gilmour)

### Side Two
Pigs (Three Different Ones) (Waters)
Sheep (Waters)
Pigs on the Wing (Part Two) (Waters)

| | |
|---|---|
| **Recorded:** | April–December, 1976, Britannia Row Studios, London |
| **Released:** | January 21, 1977 (UK), February 12, 1977 (US) |
| **Label:** | Harvest (UK), Columbia (US) |
| **Producer:** | Pink Floyd |
| **Personnel:** | David Gilmour (guitars, bass guitar, harmonica, vocals, talk box), Roger Waters (bass guitar, guitars, vocoder, vocals), Richard Wright (keyboards, ARP string synthesizer, Hammond organ, EMS VCS3, vocals), Nick Mason (drums, percussion) |
| **Additional Personnel:** | |
| | Snowy White (guitar) ["Pigs on the Wing" 8-track release only] |
| **Chart Position:** | UK No. 2, US No. 3, Germany No. 1, Italy No. 1, Netherlands No. 1, New Zealand No. 1, Spain No. 1, Norway No. 2, Austria No. 2 |

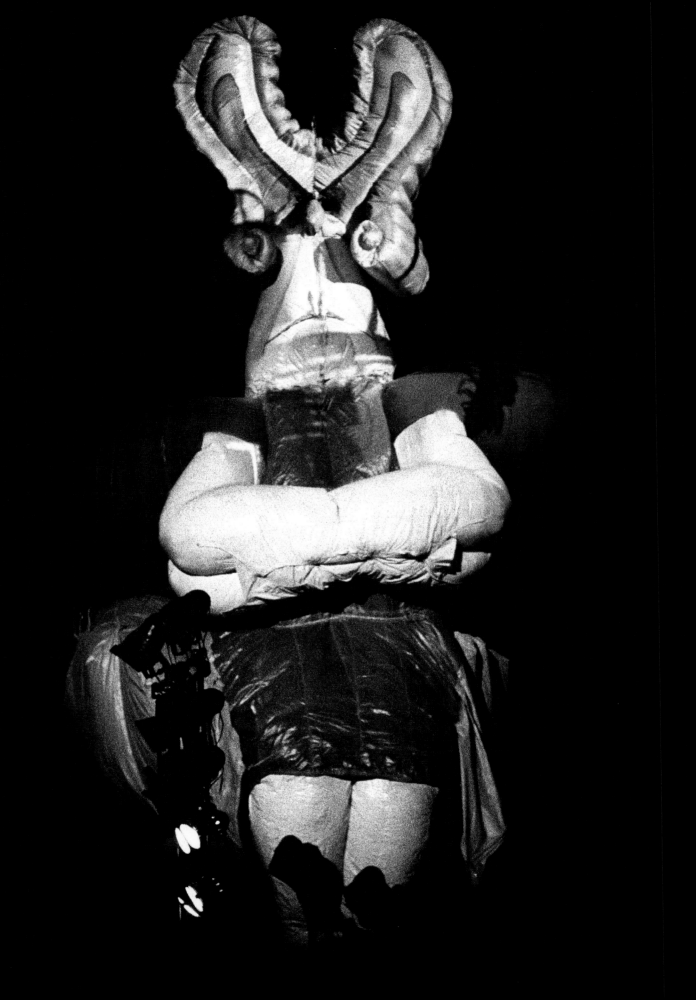

# the wall

"During that period I went a little bit mad and really dreaded going in to face the tension . . . I'd prefer not to be there while Roger was there."

**Bob Ezrin**

---

OPPOSITE: The Mother puppet appears onstage during Pink Floyd's performance at Earls Court, London, as part of the *Wall* tour, August 6, 1980

## Bricks in the Wall

**A**fter the roller-coaster ride of the 1977 American tour, with nothing planned for the immediate—or indeed long-term—future, solo activities became a predictable preoccupation for Gilmour, Wright, and Mason.

Nick Mason was the first of the trio to enter the recording studios in December 1977, when he began work as producer and engineer for the fourth album by the prog rock guitarist Steve Hillage. The album, *Green*, was released in April 1978 to favorable reviews, and has remained something of an underground classic since then. Mason had already sat in the producer's chair on several occasions prior to *Green*, not least earlier in 1977 when he produced the second long-player by punk heroes The Damned, *Music for Pleasure*.

Rick Wright cut his first solo collection at the Super Bear studios near the French Riviera resort of Nice, where Pink Floyd would later record their next album. Entitled *Wet Dream*, Wright's record featured the ex-King Crimson saxophonist Mel Collins, and guitarist Snowy White, the latter fresh from the baptism of fire that was the Floyd 1977 *Animals* tour. In terms of chart action, the album would disappear without trace after its release in September 1978.

The French studio was also the scene for David Gilmour's first solo recordings just a few weeks after the *Wet Dream* sessions. Predominantly a blues and rock-oriented album, the eponymously titled *David Gilmour* included in the line-up Gilmour's old colleagues from his days in Jokers Wild, guitarist Rick Wills and drummer Willie Wilson. Released in May '78, the album went on to make the No. 17 spot on the UK long-player charts, and No. 29 on the *Billboard* chart in the

LEFT: English prog rock guitarist Steve Hillage, whose album *Green* Nick Mason produced, pictured in 1977

USA, where it was awarded a Gold disc.

In the aftermath of the *Animals* tour, it wasn't just the various solo projects that concentrated minds. The band's finances were in a mess, and as things came to a head in 1978 they were having to pick up the pieces. Back in 1976, the group had engaged the services of a company of financial advisers, Norton Warburg. Under their auspices, in order to avoid the stunning 83 percent high earners in the UK were expected to pay in income tax at the time, the company came up with various suggestions as to what the band should do with their now-considerable fortunes. In the aftermath of *Dark Side of the Moon*, Pink Floyd were now among the biggest earners in the music business, and while enjoying the fruits of their good fortune with all the trappings of luxury lifestyles, they were attracted by any advice that lessened their tax liability.

Norton Warburg recommended that a considerable slice of the band's earnings should be invested in various venture capital enterprises. But most of these investments proved financially disastrous, involving a bizarre range of companies including a chain of pizza restaurants, a children's shoe manufacturer, a car hire business, and many other high-risk schemes. In the event Norton Warburg itself collapsed, and when the company's affairs were finally sorted out in 1981, it transpired that Pink Floyd had lost over £3 million in the process. In the summer of 1978, as the extent of their losses was becoming more and more apparent, there was even more pressure on the band to come up with some ideas for a new album.

A meeting was convened at Britannia Row in July, and it was Roger Waters who came to the rescue. Since the band had returned from touring a year earlier, while the other three had

been preoccupied with their solo projects and such, Waters had been busily preparing extensive demos of two new proposals for the next Pink Floyd album.

The incident a year earlier, when Roger spat on a member of the audience in Montreal, on the closing date of their North American tour, had obviously played on the bass player's mind over the subsequent months. He ruminated on the division he felt now existed between the band and their audience, a barrier—or indeed a "wall"—that had grown exponentially, as their fame and wealth increased beyond their wildest dreams.

By the time of the Britannia Row meeting, Roger had amassed a bunch of demo tapes to illustrate his two album concepts for consideration by the rest of the group. Initially, the others thought the demos were pretty rough; talking to author Glenn Povey in 1987, Dave Gilmour described them as "unlistenable, a shitty mess . . . you couldn't tell them apart." But gradually, Waters' proposals began to make sense as he talked through the ideas he had in mind. One prospective album, a "rock opera" called *Bricks in the Wall*, came directly out of his concerns about the alienation of their fans, triggered by the Montreal event. The other, *The Pros and Cons of Hitch Hiking*, addressed the fears and trauma of a man in mid-life crisis through a dream fantasy of an affair with a hitch-hiker. After listening to the disparate selection of demos at the meeting, and subsequent get-togethers in Roger's home studio, the band eventually opted for the *Bricks in the Wall* idea, agreeing that the *Pros and Cons of Hitch Hiking* notion (which was only supported by Steve O'Rourke) would perhaps work better as a solo excursion by Roger—which indeed it did, when he released it as such in 1984.

Through the closing months of 1978, preparations were in hand to begin recording, which all agreed would have to be for a double album. Roger Waters' original vision was for the project to appear in various media formats at the same time: The album would be supported by live concerts (supplemented by appropriate stage effects), and a cinema film release. But it very quickly became clear that the multimedia approach was far from practical, and eventually the entire project would span several years, from its initial inception in 1978 to the release of the movie in 1982. And from the start, Roger conceded that, unlike on their previous half dozen albums, Pink Floyd would not be the sole producer credited. He claimed that for this exercise he needed a sympathetic collaborator, and none of his band colleagues seemed enthusiastic enough to commit to the job.

The tensions within the band had subsided somewhat since the often chaotic tour, certainly enough for them all to concentrate their minds on their next album, but there was still an underlying friction lurking below the surface calm. Relationships were particularly sensitive between Roger and David, as they also were between Roger and Rick Wright, who had almost left the band during the American trip. Much of the angst centered on the apportionment of royalties from *Animals* (especially in the case of Gilmour's share), and a recognition that Roger was now running the band in all but name. In fairness to the bass player, who was now the de facto songwriter for Pink Floyd, at this stage he was also the only member coming up with any positive plan for the future. And Nick Mason, as always, remained a steadying influence when the quartet's partnership seemed at breaking point. Consequently, Waters' decision to seek another voice in

the production team was also in recognition that the band would benefit from an outsider's arbitration when disagreements arose.

It was Waters' then-wife, Carolyne Christie, who suggested Bob Ezrin, a time-served producer who had worked with various top names including Lou Reed (on his *Berlin* album), Alice Cooper, and most recently Peter Gabriel on his first solo outing. Carolyne had worked for Canadian Ezrin some time earlier, and had introduced him to the band when they played Hamilton, Ontario, on their last tour. But Ezrin wasn't the only new recruit to the production line-up.

The band's regular sound engineer Brian Humphries was, they all agreed, totally exhausted after working for five years with Pink Floyd. And although the in-house engineer at Britannia Row, Nick Griffiths, was considered another option, the band felt he didn't have enough experience on his side. Alan Parsons, the engineer who had been nominated for a Grammy Award for his work on *Dark Side of the Moon*, was an obvious choice, but he was now preoccupied with his own band, The Alan Parsons Project. But Parsons suggested that Pink Floyd speak to

OPPOSITE: David Gilmour's eponymous debut solo album, 1978

ABOVE: David Gilmour at Britannia Row Studios, London, 1978

# "I saw myself as a hot young *producer*... when we [Guthrie and Ezrin] arrived, I think we both felt we'd been booked to do the same job."

## James Guthrie

a relative unknown, James Guthrie. The recommended engineer, who had actually been working with the metal band Judas Priest among others, was offered a production role after a minimal audition and interview with Steve O'Rourke and Waters. The two failed to make clear to the new recruit that the job would be as a "co-producer," omitting to explain that he would be sharing the role with Bob Ezrin, thus creating some initial confusion: "I saw myself as a hot young *producer*," Guthrie recalled, "... when we [Guthrie and Ezrin] arrived, I think we both felt we'd been booked to do the same job." Roger Waters, ever at the helm, couldn't be left out of the creative decision-making process, and along with Dave Gilmour completed the production credit as Ezrin, Waters, Gilmour, and Guthrie.

## Storyline to Studio

Essential to the whole album's concept was Roger Waters' already envisaged storyline, which would form the backbone and structure of the entire work. Based on the personalities of both himself and Pink Floyd's erstwhile front man Syd Barrett, Waters' central character is a rock star, significantly named Pink. The anti-hero protagonist has a troubled, fatherless childhood, with an overprotective mother and abusive experiences at school, which sees him building a metaphorical wall around himself from an early age. Into adulthood and fame, Pink marries, only to cheat on his wife (who also proves unfaithful in his absence) while on tour. In his ensuing guilt-ridden isolation, locked in his hotel room and refusing human contact, Pink finalizes the "wall" he has been seemingly constructing throughout his life.

Reality kicks in when Pink's manager and road crew break into his room, where they find him unconscious. Drugs are administered so he can take to the stage that evening, and he performs the ensuing gig in a state of extreme hallucination. Imagining himself as some sort of fascist dictator in front of a Nazi-like rally, his military henchmen set upon any fans he

disapproves of. More fantasized violence ensues at another rally, set in London, before the hallucinating comes to an end. Pink then seeks redemption via his inner conscience, that concludes he should "tear down the wall."

Bob Ezrin, for one, was quick to recognize the significance of the storyline as presented in Waters' lyrics, and made his own contribution to their fine-tuning as the project developed. Roger had initially written the songs in the first person, but the producer felt it should move away from being purely autobiographical: "If you looked at the original lyrics, Roger was being very honest about his fear and pain and isolation. But when we turned him into Pink, we were able to give him even more fear, pain, and isolation."

After almost six months of preparation, during which the rambling collection of Roger's home demos had been gradually honed to workable outlines for a double album, in December 1978, Pink Floyd were ready to begin work on what would be their eleventh studio release in a dozen years.

Initial sessions took place at Britannia Row, but in the early months of 1979, their accountants—who had all but occupied the band's office space since the extent of the Norton Warburg debacle became clear—advised they should become tax exiles. This would involve the four, and their families, moving residency out of the United Kingdom for at least a year, whereby any earnings in that period would not be subject to tax. The deadline for such a move, to avoid total bankruptcy, was April 6, the start of the next taxable year.

The moves were made, with the band booking time in Super Bear, a studio complex near Nice in the South of France, where both Rick and David had cut their debut albums a few months earlier. All the band had second homes in mainland Europe, so family accommodation seemed to be no problem. And for the purposes of working at Super Bear, Mason and Wright stayed at the well-appointed studio itself, while Gilmour and Waters rented houses nearby.

Things in the studio, perhaps inevitably, didn't run smoothly from the start. Bob Ezrin soon irritated the others, especially Roger Waters, by his lack of punctuality. Ensconced in the luxurious Hotel Negresco in Nice, the Canadian also grew resentful of his lower share of the royalties, and Waters' "bullying" attitude over the issue. "During that period I went a little bit mad and really dreaded going in to face the tension," he would recall. "I'd prefer not to be there while Roger was there."

Recording time was also booked at the Miraval Studios in Correns, fifty miles from Nice in the Le Val area. The new schedule was to run parallel with the Super Bear sessions, after CBS had offered to increase the band's percentage if they delivered the completed album in time for a release date at the end of the year. This brought new pressure to bear on the personnel, affecting individuals in various ways. Nick Mason would admit that he was "let off quite lightly," having laid down the drum tracks early on in the process at Super Bear. Waters, Gilmour, and Wright, meanwhile, were rarely working at the same time in the studios, with Ezrin and James Guthrie sharing their production duties between the two locations.

Things really came to a head between Roger Waters and Rick Wright after the revised work itinerary was agreed with CBS. The band had scheduled a holiday break for August, reconvening in Los Angeles to resume recording in September; now any plans for a summer vacation had to be postponed, and for Wright this posed a particular dilemma. Rick had been going through some marriage problems as it was, exacerbated by the "tax exile" situation. With his children at school, the enforced absence couldn't simply include the family on every occasion, and an already shaky marriage was now in a critical phase. When told he had to put any domestic plans on hold, in order to complete the still-to-be-recorded keyboard parts, Rick Wright simply refused.

Roger Waters was furious. He, and the other two members of Pink Floyd, already felt that Rick's contribution to the album up until then had been minimal, and now the crunch had come. According to Nick Mason's account of events, Waters rang Steve O'Rourke—who was on his way to New York on the *QE2* at the time—and ordered the manager to sack Rick immediately. Dave Gilmour, who was enjoying a short break in Dublin, tried to patch things up when he learned of Rick's pending dismissal.

OPPOSITE: Rehearsing ahead of Pink Floyd's Earls Court concert, August 1980

RIGHT: Jeff Porcaro, who played drums on "Mother"

Roger's final ultimatum, threatening to refuse the album's release otherwise, was for Rick to cease being an actual member of Pink Floyd after *The Wall* was released, but play as a paid session musician on forthcoming concerts supporting the album. (Ironically, the arrangement meant that Rick was the only one of the four who would actually make any money from the loss-making live extravaganzas.)

So, as the band attended to the subsequently delayed final recording and mixing in various studios—at CBS in New York, followed by Cherokee Studios, the Village Recorder, and the Producers' Workshop in Los Angeles—*The Wall*, released on the last day of November 1979, was potentially the last Pink Floyd album to feature Richard Wright, one of the founding members of the quartet.

## The Album

With a total of twenty-six tracks, the epic sweep of the album's concept was evident in the track listing on the four-sided vinyl release. But most songs were kept to an economically minimal length, avoiding the expansive indulgences that had characterized the band's previous two long-players.

The autobiographical nature of the whole work is quickly established following the strident guitar chords that announce "In the Flesh?," giving way almost immediately to Roger's flashback

reference (as "Pink") to his father's death in World War II. Complete with the sound of enemy dive-bombers, at just over three minutes in, the sound of an infant crying segues into "The Thin Ice." David Gilmour's plaintive lullaby vocal is quickly followed by more of Pink's ruminations via Roger, before we find ourselves in the (now) more familiar territory of "Another Brick in the Wall."

Part 1 of the album's key anthem, firmly introduced by Waters' insistent bass, has Pink asking what his deceased father's sacrifice was meant to achieve for his infant son. It's a despondent plea that can't be answered; a doom-laden conclusion, in a minor key, that his father's death is, indeed, the first brick in the wall. A short track preceded by the sound of a helicopter briefly outlines Pink's rage against the educational machine, with memories of corporal punishment and worse. The deliberate irony of the title, "The Happiest Days of Our Lives," says it all—and this is, indeed, "Another Brick in the Wall."

The second part of the signature song would be the band's biggest-ever hit single. Railing against education, mind control, the sarcastic attitude of teachers, and the plea to "leave us kids alone"—on the second time around voiced by an actual choir of children from Islington Green School in London—it hit a nerve. The disco beat of the backing for Part 2 was the brainchild of Bob Ezrin, after being inspired by the success of producer Nile Rodgers and others on the New York disco scene. It was also Ezrin's idea to add the kids' choir, convinced the band could have a chart hit

> **"If you looked at the original lyrics, Roger was being very honest about his fear and pain and isolation. But when we turned him into Pink, we were able to give him even more fear, pain, and isolation."**
>
> **Bob Ezrin**

on their hands. At first Pink Floyd resisted the idea, insisting they weren't a "singles band"—their last single had been "Point Me at the Sky" in 1968—but they eventually acquiesced. Which was just as well: Released on the same day as the album, the single hit the top of the charts in the UK, US, and no less than a dozen other countries. In Britain it was the Christmas No. 1 single for 1979 and went on to sell over four million copies worldwide.

One of the longer tracks on the collection, and the finale to the first side of the vinyl set, "Mother" features a powerful quartet consisting of Waters on bass and vocals, Dave Gilmour, Bob Ezrin on piano, and session guest Jeff Porcaro on drums. Seemingly Nick Mason found the tricky time signatures difficult to master, given the tight schedule they were working to. In this instance Waters' lyrics are not directly reflecting his own experience, having had a positive relationship with his own mother, but a consideration of the possibilities of over-protective parenthood—here presented in the context of his fictional alter ego, Pink. Again, it's a case for another brick to be added to an ever-growing wall.

A child's voice (Roger Waters' small son Harry did the honors in the studio) declares "Look mummy, there's an aeroplane up in the sky," as the sound of approaching warplanes preludes a poignant ballad. With a delicate acoustic backing, David Gilmour sings "Goodbye Blue Sky," the short evocation of Pink's disturbed memories of a wartime childhood. It's followed by the unnerving link of "Empty Spaces," full of sinister-sounding effects and hard-to-decipher conversations, before we're transported to the adult reality of Pink the rock star.

"Young Lust" evokes the hard-edged world of rock on the road, as Pink engages with a groupie, only to learn of his wife's infidelity back in England, via an international phone call. It's definitely Gilmour-driven Floyd, with the guitarist at his majestic best.

David co-wrote the song with Roger, and it shows—not least in his confident delivery of the knowing vocal lines. Pink's behavior becomes more overwrought in "One of My Turns," however, after he takes the girl back to his hotel, only to ignore her advances and instead violently trashes the room. The track shifts from introspective reflections by Pink (gently voiced by Waters) to a nihilistic bombardment of the senses, before he despondently screams: "Why are you running away?" The track would appear as the (somewhat unlikely) B-side to the hit single of "Another Brick in the Wall (Part 2)."

A desolate plea for sympathy from a man at the end of his tether, Roger delivers Pink's heartfelt soliloquy "Don't Leave Me Now" with a distanced passion. It's a lonely, isolated voice begging to be heard by those around him, who he's often treated with a selfish disregard. With his self-created isolation now virtually complete, in "Another Brick in the Wall (Part 3)," Pink retreats into his delusion that this is the answer. Almost defiantly, he declares that he doesn't need "anything at all," backed by the familiar theme now delivered with a darker edge than previously. And with the wall around himself completed, in "Goodbye Cruel World" Pink delivers a mournful, almost funereal farewell, that could well have been a tragic ending to the entire narrative. Roger spells out the solitary message accompanied only by his bass, and Rick Wright's synthesizer—a chillingly stark closure to the first half of a monumental saga.

Now trapped in the confines of his wall, Pink's plea to the outside world can no longer be heard. A languorous acoustic opening soon explodes into a spectacular performance by Dave Gilmour, who shares the vocals on "Hey You" with Roger Waters. One of the most dynamic songs on the album, it serves to confirm the increasing loneliness of Pink's situation.

Against the sinister-sounding background of a TV drama, Roger/Pink appeals to anyone who will listen: "Is There Anybody Out There?"—the title of a short piece highlighted by a sparse classical Spanish guitar accompaniment by Joe DiBlasi. The session musician was brought in when Gilmour decided he couldn't achieve the result he wanted: "I could play it with a leather pick, but couldn't play it properly fingerstyle," he would admit. The evocative synthesizer and violin backing was arranged by Michael Kamen, the accomplished composer and arranger brought in on Ezrin's suggestion to add some orchestral texture to a number of the tracks.

"Nobody Home" was the first track in the running order to feature a full classical ensemble, the New York Symphony Orchestra, courtesy of Kamen. With some thinly veiled visual references to Syd Barrett ("wild, staring eyes," "Hendrix perm," and such), it's a stark image of the stereotypical wasted rock star, personified in Waters' character Pink. There's some powerful piano provided by Bob Ezrin to underscore Roger's sonorous vocal, before the strings kick in bringing a certain majesty to the proceedings. The track was born late in the album's creation, at the Producers' Workshop in L.A. in October. Seemingly, Gilmour had challenged Waters to write something, with the latter leaving the session "in a sulk," only to return the next day with a small masterpiece. All the string parts for the album, including "Nobody Home," were added at the CBS studios in New York City; at that stage Michael Kamen had yet to deal with the band face to face, only actually meeting them when the sessions were finished.

Unashamed nostalgia on the part of Pink (and of course Waters himself) characterizes the two short tracks "Vera" and "Bring the Boys Back Home." The first, in homage to the World War II "forces sweetheart," singer Vera Lynn, recalls Pink's early childhood and his father's death. With an emotive strings and brass backing, Waters rehashes the delivery of Vera's most famous hit, "We'll Meet Again," before launching into an angrier tirade. "Bring the Boys Back Home" conjures up the notion of families demanding the return of their sons from the battlefront, to the calamitous soundtrack of the New York City Opera and a unison marching rhythm provided by thirty-six snare-drummers.

ABOVE LEFT: Composer Michael Kamen, who added some orchestral texture to *The Wall*

ABOVE RIGHT: Lee Ritenour, who contributed acoustic guitar on "Comfortably Numb"

A definite high point of the double album, "Comfortably Numb" represents a marker in both the Pink saga, and David Gilmour's often fractured relationship with Roger Waters. Pertaining to Pink, the lyrics refer to the star's manager, panicking that he might have to pull that night's concert, having the comatose singer injected with drugs to enable him to perform. In the real world of Roger Waters' own experience, it also recalled an instance in Philadelphia during Pink Floyd's 1977 US tour, when he had to be sedated against hepatitis-related stomach cramps in order to go onstage.

Simply one of the finest recordings in the entire Floyd songbook, "Comfortably Numb" represents David Gilmour at his best as a collaborative singer and songwriter. The deceptively no-frills, blues-tinged guitar solos lift the song to a majestic place, aided in no small degree by the presence of the strings of the New York Symphony Orchestra, and Lee Ritenour guesting on acoustic guitar.

The recording would see the Floyd guitarist and bass player yet again at odds over what many would judge as mere details. Although the basic composition was a painless—and ultimately hugely successful—joint effort between the two, arguments ensued over the mixing, and which of two recorded versions they should use. Waters advocated the orchestral arrangement, while Gilmour favored a more basic, pared-down version. "We had

another go at it, and I thought that the second take was better," the guitarist remembered. "Roger disagreed. It was more an ego thing than anything else. We really went head to head with each other over such a minor thing. I probably couldn't tell the difference if you put both versions on a record today. But anyway, it wound up with us taking a fill out of one version and putting it into another." David Gilmour later went on to say that it was the last occasion when he and Roger Waters were able to successfully work together.

Into the final side of the original track listing, we have Pink—propped up by the "medication" he's been administered—making a half-conscious, psychedelically driven appearance onstage. With harmonic touches hinting at classic-period Beach Boys, Gilmour's vocals handle the slight, short melody of "The Show Must Go On" with aplomb. But as soon as the minute-and-a-half song is over, we're into far more sinister territory as Pink fantasizes his role as a fascist dictator, ordering the persecution of "undesirable" members of the audience. From Gilmour's opening tirade of aggressive flourishes, "In the Flesh"—apart from the vocals, a rerun of the album's opener—is a stunning piece of musical theater despite the depressing nature of the lyrics.

Co-written by Gilmour and Waters, "Run Like Hell" continues Pink's litany of hate, as he urges the mob against the background of a militaristic, unrelenting beat. It's a hypnotic tirade which gestates

into the equally disturbing "Waiting for the Worms," despite the track being far less mechanically strident than its immediate predecessor. The nightmare delirium on the part of Pink finally dissipates into the monotonous chanting of his followers, before the hallucination comes to an end. "Stop," a simple plea accompanied by a minimalistic piano courtesy of Bob Ezrin, has Pink awaking from his dystopian reveries in a police cell, awaiting his self-judgment in "The Trial."

For the penultimate song, Waters and Ezrin came up with a quasi-humorous, camp take on the plot. Pink faces his trial before a musical montage of his accusers, set against an orchestral arrangement by Ezrin, performed by the New York Symphony Orchestra. With more than a nod to the theatrics of *Cabaret* (and its inspiration, the pre-war German *Threepenny Opera* by Bertolt Brecht and Kurt Weill), it's a grotesque-sounding parade of Pink's inner voices; voices now calling for the destruction of the wall.

As we hear the wall finally collapsing, on "Outside the Wall" Roger (as Pink) recites a concluding verse to a simple pastoral accompaniment of concertina and clarinet. He's conceding that the wall is always there, as a continuous structure without a beginning or end. To confirm the notion, the disembodied voice concluding the work, abruptly cut off, utters "Isn't this where," linking with the album's equally scant opening phrase, twenty-six tracks earlier, ". . . we came in?"

OPPOSITE: Artist Gerald Scarfe in his studio, 1982

ABOVE: Pink Floyd perform live onstage at Earls Court, London, during the *Wall* tour, August 6, 1980

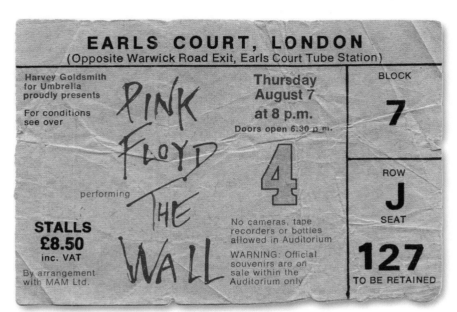

EARLS COURT, LONDON
(Opposite Warwick Road Exit, Earls Court Tube Station)

Harvey Goldsmith
for Umbrella
proudly presents

For conditions
see over

PINK
FLOYD

performing

THE
WALL

STALLS
£8.50
inc. VAT

By arrangement
with MAM Ltd.

Thursday
August 7
at 8 p.m.
Doors open 6.30 p.m.

4

No cameras, tape
recorders or bottles
allowed in Auditorium

WARNING: Official
souvenirs are on
sale within the
Auditorium only

BLOCK
7

ROW
J

SEAT
127

TO BE RETAINED

## On Sale

*The Wall* would be the first Pink Floyd album since the band's 1967 debut LP, *The Piper at the Gates of Dawn*, not to have a cover designed by the Hipgnosis team. This time the sleeve art was the work of the cartoonist and illustrator Gerald Scarfe, who had created the center spread for the band's 1974–75 tour program, and more recently the back-projected animations featured on the *Animals* tour in 1977.

Scarfe had risen to prominence in the 1960s, when his caricatures of politicians and other public figures were featured in a variety of UK newspapers and periodicals, including the satirical magazine *Private Eye*. He was approached by Roger Waters and Nick Mason after the pair watched his eighteen-minute animated film for BBC TV's *Long Drawn-Out Trip*, on its one and only broadcast in 1973. Scarfe recalled how the band then used his imagery onstage, on an ad hoc basis: "Apparently the guys saw this on TV here in Britain, and Roger said to Nick, 'We've got to have this guy on board. He's fucking mad!' So that's how I got introduced to the group. And thereafter I did small bits of animation for them, which I took almost daily to their gigs. I did a little bit of animation—more likely weekly, I guess—and they'd just kind of jam it in wherever they'd think it'd work."

The illustration for the sleeve was in stark contrast to the band's previous packaging. While the Hipgnosis designs were marked by an almost surreal use of photography—even the lone cow displayed on *Atom Heart Mother* was an oddity in itself, in the context of an album illustration—all *The Wall* displayed was simply that, a plain white brick wall with no information whatsoever.

ABOVE: Ticket for a Pink Floyd concert at Earls Court, London, August 7, 1980

LEFT: The Teacher puppet appears onstage

## "There can only be one place to line up tax-exile millionaires who make concept albums about what a terrible hand life has dealt them ... UP AGAINST THE WALL."

### *Sounds* Magazine

The album title and Pink Floyd's name appeared variously as a sticker, or on sleeve wrapping, or (later) on the cover itself. These were in a specific script designed by Scarfe in the artist's trademark style, and from there on appeared in various visual contexts associated with the band—including, of course, the ongoing manifestations of *The Wall* on stage and screen.

Gerald Scarfe also designed all the interior packaging for the vinyl double album, showing the wall at different stages of construction, with (usually grotesque) characters from the plot. These exaggerated caricatures would later appear onstage during the *Wall* tour, in the form of giant dolls, and as animated characters in the subsequent film based on the album.

Not for the first time, a new album by Pink Floyd would be met by less than universal acclaim—not, at least, by the rock music critics and music press pundits. Dave McCullough wrote a particularly scathing review in *Sounds* magazine, sub-headlining the article: "There can only be one place to line up tax-exile millionaires who make concept albums about what a terrible hand life has dealt them ... UP AGAINST THE WALL." But while conceding "it in no way endangers the meisterwerk musical status of *Dark Side of the Moon*" in *Rolling Stone*, Kurt Loder called it "the most startling rhetorical achievement in the group's singular, thirteen-year career."

And the album's long-term rating among the rock cognoscenti has been reflected in its accepted place in the portals of various "Halls of Fame" and suchlike. As the highly regarded *500 Greatest Albums of All Time*, published by *Rolling Stone*, recorded in the first such listing in 2003: "Rock's ultimate self-pity opera, *The Wall* is also hypnotic in its indulgence: the totalitarian thunder of 'In the Flesh?' the suicidal languor of 'Comfortably Numb,' the Brechtian drama of 'The Trial.' Rock-star hubris has never been more electrifying."

The album's success in the record stores was immediate, however. As the concurrent single "Another Brick in the Wall (Part 2)" shot up the charts—to hit the No. 1 spot in both the US and the UK—the album would be the band's first to top the US best-sellers, where it stayed for fifteen weeks. While making

the No. 3 spot in the UK, the long-player also topped the lists in another ten nations around the globe.

## On Stage, On Screen

Perhaps predictably, when *The Wall* went on tour two months after the album release, relationships within the band were at an all-time low.

Rick Wright, as per his dismissal by Roger Waters, filled his position in the line-up as a jobbing session man. Both Nick Mason and David Gilmour went along with the situation, although both ostensibly showing more compassion to Rick than Waters had, while agreeing that the keyboard man had hardly pulled his weight during the album's creation. "I did point out to Rick that he hadn't contributed anything of any value whatsoever to the album," Gilmour later explained to *Mojo* magazine, "... and

that I wasn't over-happy with him myself."

And the rift between Gilmour and Waters, which had come to a head more than once in the recording studio over the last few months, showed no sign of healing as the tour opened with a week of concerts at the Los Angeles Memorial Sports Arena, on February 7, 1980. The L.A. dates were followed by five consecutive days in the last week of February at the Nassau Veterans Memorial Coliseum, in the Long Island suburbs of New York City. In fact the tensions between all four were apparent in their backstage arrangements; each musician had his own Portakabin as dressing room, and famously the four would park them in a circle, with the doors facing outwards from the center. On other occasions, Roger Waters would use his own car to arrive at locations, often staying at separate hotels from the other three. And according to Nick Mason, they would even stage their own individual after-show parties. The concerts were guaranteed sell-outs, so much so that the band were offered a million dollars to play two extra dates in Philadelphia—but Roger, again in a clear confrontation with the rest of the band, insisted they didn't do it.

ABOVE: The *Wall* tour continues with a backdrop of projected animation, Earls Court, London, June 16, 1981

To call the stage show spectacular would be a gross understatement. Reflecting Waters' fixation on the barrier he perceived between the band and their audience—the key theme of the album—a gigantic 12-meter-high wall was built during the first half of the performance, gradually separating Pink Floyd from their fans. The huge "bricks" in the wall were made of cardboard, easily folded flat for transportation, and erected by the road crew as the set progressed. There were 340 such "bricks" on the completion of the wall, which was used during the performance to show portions of the animated film made by Gerald Scarfe in addition to three Scarfe-designed giant inflatable puppets representing the sadistic Schoolteacher, Pink's mother, and his unfaithful ex-wife.

But perhaps the most bizarre element in the production was the appearance of a "fake" Pink Floyd right at the start of the performance. The "surrogate band" would open each show, rising from beneath the stage, and wearing prosthetic masks of the particular Floyd member they represented. As the opening song, "In the Flesh," concluded, the surrogate group would freeze, the real Floyd emerging from behind them. Among well-known musicians in the fake personnel (who also played alongside the real Floyd during the performance) were guitarist Snowy White, who had augmented the line-up on the In the Flesh tour, and keyboards man Andy Bown, later to be a full-time member of the rock band Status Quo.

Due to the challenging logistics involved in staging the shows, the blocks of concerts were few and far between, with the only other dates in 1980 being six concerts in August, at London's Earls Court Exhibition Hall. These were followed in 1981 by eight February shows in Dortmund, West Germany, and in June six final presentations of *The Wall*, again at Earls Court, London. Most of the paying customers at the events were stunned by the show, almost regardless of the 106-decibel quadraphonic music, which the majority were familiar with anyway. And almost all reviews of the concerts concluded that the theatrical extravaganza was foremost in the experience, as the scribe in the UK music paper *Sounds* reported on the Los Angeles show: "The only problem is that the whole business is so perfectly organised that you end up being more concerned with the strings than what they're pulling. It's all so complex, so perfectly choreographed that it makes you numb as well. You spend more time worrying that something is going to go wrong than enjoying the show."

The third phase of Roger Waters' ambitious plan for the *Wall* project was the movie, which went into production a few months after the concerts wound up in June 1981. Entitled *Pink Floyd: The Wall*, the film was directed by the renowned British filmmaker Alan Parker, and featured Bob Geldof as Pink. The film was originally intended to feature animated scenes between

concert footage, but when the latter approach proved impractical to shoot, Parker decided to use actors (with little or no dialogue) between the animations.

Once again Gerald Scarfe's creations were key to the animated segments, which he directed, with his larger-than-life caricatures even more grotesque than their manifestations onstage. Sequences like Scarfe's "marching hammers" became part of the memorable iconography associated with the entire *Wall* trilogy: in promotional videos for the album, the onstage animations, and now a movie.

The film was shown at the Cannes Film Festival in May 1982, prior to its official premiere in London on July 14. The

three remaining members of Pink Floyd attended the screening, with Richard Wright now not being an actual member of the band. The movie was received with generally positive reviews by the critics, and went on to be nominated for two BAFTA awards—including one for Best Original Song, for Roger Waters' "Another Brick in the Wall."

By the time of the film's release, Pink Floyd—after a long absence from the recording studio—were about to embark on work for their next album. Originally planned as the soundtrack for the *Wall* movie, *The Final Cut* would be the only album by the band not to feature their founding member keyboard player Rick Wright, and the last album to feature fellow-founder Roger Waters. Like *The Wall* at its spectacular finale, as they prepared to go into the studio again in July 1982, the band seemed to be crumbling as the world looked on.

ABOVE: More projected animations at Earls Court, London, 1981

# The Wall

Track Listing (original UK vinyl release)

## Side One

In the Flesh? (Roger Waters)
The Thin Ice (Waters)
Another Brick in the Wall (Part 1) (Waters)
The Happiest Days of Our Lives (Waters)
Another Brick in the Wall (Part 2) (Waters)
Mother (Waters)

## Side Two

Goodbye Blue Sky (Waters)
Empty Spaces (Waters)
Young Lust (Waters, David Gilmour)
One of My Turns (Waters)
Don't Leave Me Now (Waters)
Another Brick in the Wall (Part 3) (Waters)
Goodbye Cruel World (Waters)

## Side Three

Hey You (Waters)
Is There Anybody Out There? (Waters)
Nobody Home (Waters)
Vera (Waters)
Bring the Boys Back Home (Waters)
Comfortably Numb (Gilmour, Waters)

## Side Four

The Show Must Go On (Waters)
In the Flesh (Waters)
Run Like Hell (Gilmour, Waters)
Waiting for the Worms (Waters)
Stop (Waters)
The Trial (Waters, Bob Ezrin)
Outside the Wall (Waters)

**Recorded:** December 1978 – November 1979, Britannia Row Studios, London; Super Bear Studios, Nice, France; Miraval Studios, Correns, France; CBS 30th Street Studio, New York; Cherokee Studios, Hollywood; Village Recorder, Los Angeles; Producers' Workshop, Los Angeles

**Released:** November 30, 1979

**Label:** Harvest (UK), Columbia (US)

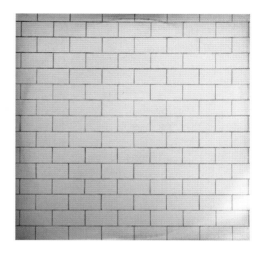

**Producer:** Bob Ezrin, David Gilmour, James Guthrie, Roger Waters

**Personnel:** Roger Waters (bass guitar, EMS VCS3, guitars, vocals), David Gilmour (guitars, bass guitar, synthesizers, vocals), Richard Wright (Hammond organ, synthesizers, piano, keyboards, clavinet), Nick Mason (drums, percussion)

**Additional Personnel:**
Bob Ezrin (piano, Hammond organ, harmonium, synthesizer, backing vocals), James Guthrie (percussion, synthesizer), Fred Mandel (Hammond organ), Jeff Porcaro (drums), Lee Ritenour (guitars), Joe (Ron) di Blasi (guitar), Bobbye Hall (percussion), Frank Marocco (concertina), Larry Williams (clarinet), Trevor Veitch (mandolin), New York Symphony Orchestra (orchestra), New York Opera (choral vocals), Bruce Johnston, Toni Tenille, Joe Chemay, Jon Joyce, Stan Farber, Jim Haas, Islington Green School children, Harry Waters, Trudy Young, Vicki Brown, Clare Torry (backing vocals)

**Chart Position:** US No. 1, UK No. 3, Australia No. 1, Austria No. 1, Canada No. 1, Germany No. 1, Italy No. 1, Netherlands No. 1, New Zealand No. 1, Norway No. 1, Spain No. 1, Sweden No. 1

# the final cut

"It may be that in Roger's head he was already moving into a solo career, and merely wanted David and me to assist him in his aspirations."

**Nick Mason**

## Recess, Reunion

In the absence of what record companies insisted on calling "product," after the 1979 release of *The Wall*, devoted Floyd fans had to make do with just two albums linked in some way to the band before their next major release in 1983, both records appearing in 1981.

In May of that year, just prior to the last of the sporadic *Wall* concerts, EMI-Harvest released *Nick Mason's Fictitious Sports*. Recorded back in October 1979 at the end of the *Wall* sessions, it was the drummer's first solo album, and by his own admission something he "made more as an exercise." The exercise in

question, recorded in Woodstock in upstate New York, involved the distinguished jazz composer and keyboard player Carla Bley, with ex-Soft Machine drummer Robert Wyatt delivering all the vocals, and Mason on drums. Other luminaries on the recordings, which featured just songs written by Bley, included Chris Spedding on guitar, Steve Swallow on bass, and Bley's then-husband, trumpeter Michael Mantler. But despite Nick's name featuring in the actual title of the release, it failed to make a great impression sales-wise, peaking at just No. 170 in the American album chart.

Then in November 1981, the record company put together the

Harvest and Capitol Records in the US. Gilmour played guitars, keyboards, bass, and drums on the track, with Dick Parry (who'd guested on the *Dark Side of the Moon* original) on saxophone. Perhaps surprisingly, for what amounted to a lackluster release for Floyd followers starved of fresh material, it actually sold quite well, hitting No. 31 and No. 37 in the US and UK, respectively. Interestingly, the cover design for the collection was credited to TCP, the pseudonym for Hipgnosis, despite Roger Waters' fractured relationship with Storm Thorgerson and his team.

A few weeks after the premiere of *The Wall* film, in July 1982, Pink Floyd reconvened in the recording studio following their prolonged recess. It was the first time since the final mixing for *The Wall* album in November 1979 that the band had gotten together to record some new music. The original concept, predictably the brainchild of Roger Waters, had been a soundtrack album for the film itself, with new material recorded specifically for the movie. The original working title was "Spare Bricks," and some additional songs were planned to develop further the narrative of *The Wall*. That was all to change, however, as Waters' initial focus shifted into what amounted to an anti-war protest album.

The catalyst for the change in emphasis on Roger's part was the Falklands War, the ten-week conflict between Great Britain and Argentina which many—including Waters—felt was overtly nationalistic, and unnecessary. The album was provisionally called *A Requiem for the Post War Dream*, which was retained as the subtitle when it was released as *The Final Cut*.

Waters dedicated the work to his father, Eric, who had died in action during World War II, and explained how it was a lament for the hopes for a better world, following that conflict, which were never fully realized.

Waters' adjustment in the overall direction immediately became a crucial area of conflict with David Gilmour, who felt the central message of the album was now too political. Also, Roger suddenly expressed an urgency in getting the job done, and—whether intentional or not—imposed a notional deadline for the recording process, which effectively nullified any prospects of new songs from Gilmour. "I'm not sure that this was a conscious

ironically titled *A Collection of Great Dance Songs*. It was certainly not a "greatest hits" package by any means, the band's avoidance of single releases over the years making that almost impossible. The collection—the first such release since *Relics* in 1971—was an ill-considered compilation of oddments drawn from *Meddle* onwards. As well as straight reissues of "One of These Days" from *Meddle*, "Sheep" from *Animals*, and "Wish You Were Here," the album featured remixed versions of "Shine On You Crazy Diamond," and "Another Brick in the Wall (Part 2)." Plus there was a completely new, re-recorded take on "Money," a makeover created by Dave Gilmour in response to a dispute between EMI/

LEFT: David Gilmour, 1982

OPPOSITE: Chris Spedding (left) and jazz musician Carla Bley (right) who appeared on Nick Mason's debut solo album, *Nick Mason's Fictitious Sports*

## "I came off the production credits because my ideas weren't the way Roger saw it. It is not personally how I would see a Pink Floyd record going."

## David Gilmour

power play by Roger," Nick Mason would later write. "I suspect that he might have been angry or simply impatient . . . or it may be that in Roger's head he was already moving into a solo career, and merely wanted David and me to assist him in his aspirations."

Confirming in many respects the fragmentation that had occurred within the Pink Floyd ranks, rehearsals and recording for the album were conducted in eight separate studios, in and around London—often with the three band members similarly dispersed. Although the apparent friction between Gilmour and Waters appeared to have calmed down as the sessions commenced—for a while the pair spent their "between takes" spare time together, playing the *Donkey Kong* video game—they were soon choosing to work apart. Their long-standing studio engineer James Guthrie supervised

Gilmour's guitar parts, while engineer Andy Jackson worked with Waters on his vocals.

As well as looking after the orchestral additions, Michael Kamen was also a co-producer, and, in the absence of the sacked Rick Wright, supplied various keyboard parts. Andy Bown, who'd been one of the "surrogate Floyd" group at the *Wall* concerts, also contributed on Hammond organ, while Nick Mason's drum part was supplemented by the star percussionist Ray Cooper on one track, and Andy Newmark (another "ex-surrogate") on another. Indeed, much of Mason's contribution was limited to recording sound effects of various kinds. Clearly, Roger Waters, being very much at the helm of the project in almost all respects, was able to pursue his creative ambitions without his former colleagues, should he so choose. At the time, Nick Mason had the more important distraction of a marriage crisis to deal with, while David Gilmour's relationship with Waters was becoming increasingly strained by the day. In the words of one chronicler, "It's perhaps surprising the record wasn't formally declared a Roger Waters solo album."

With Kamen frequently acting as a go-between, Roger and David (with Nick often a hapless observer) managed to struggle through the recording, despite what was certainly the most fractious period in their long partnership. Arguments raged constantly over the album's quality and content, to the point, according to Gilmour, that Waters was simply not interested in anyone else suggesting material. Roger would admit that they were all "fighting like cats and dogs . . . finally realizing—or accepting, of you like—that there was no band, and had not been a band in accord for a long time." Indeed, the guitarist's stance, regarding both the politics and general feel of the album, became so uncomfortable that he had his name removed from the production credits on the sleeve: "I came off the production credits because my ideas weren't the way Roger saw it. It is not personally how I would see a Pink Floyd record going." Nevertheless, Gilmour would continue to receive the appropriate royalties, on an album that many thought would be Pink Floyd's last.

## Requiem

From its opening sound of radio news soundbites, *The Final Cut* establishes the current-events basis of much of the lyrics. "The Post War Dream" is the mourning of a fast-disappearing working-class culture, embodied in the announcement of a

Japanese company getting the contract to build the next UK warship. Roger delivers poignant-sounding vocals, backed by Michael Kamen's arrangement of horns, strings, and a harmonium—the latter giving a Salvation Army hymn-like quality to the proceedings. In the song he alludes to the then-prime minister, Margaret Thatcher, by her popular nickname of "Maggie." But many present-day listeners would be more shocked by his reference to Japanese people as "Nips," a derogatory term which was still commonplace back in the 1980s.

The album consisted of a number of songs already recorded but unused from *The Wall* sessions, including the second track, "Your Possible Pasts." Waters' stark vocals evoke some disturbing images, including a reference to the Holocaust and the fate of a lone prostitute. It's a dark litany of grim notions, matched by doom-laden music featuring acoustic guitar and organ, relieved (if that's the right word) by some equally bleak soloing from Gilmour. The sense of unstated apprehension persists with another *Wall* cast-off, "One of the Few." With Waters accompanied by his own acoustic guitar, the World War II bomber pilot of the title is lamented as he returns to the post-war reality of an unfulfilled future, bitterly settling for the role of schoolteacher. It's a resentment which, as all those familiar with Waters' *Wall* view of the world know only too well, will be taken out on the pupils in his charge.

OPPOSITE: Vintage two-track single sleeve for music from *The Wall*, 1982

ABOVE: Director Alan Parker with Bob Geldof on the set of *Pink Floyd: The Wall*, 1982

There's more of a rock 'n' roll feel to "The Hero's Return," a continuation of the former airman's soliloquy as he berates his pupils, then mourns the loss of an aircrew comrade to his (significantly, sleeping) wife. Instrumentally, Gilmour's guitar is the dominant essential in this reinvention of *The Wall*'s schoolteacher villain as an erstwhile hero. And the saga continues in "The Gunner's Dream," as Waters laments the unfulfilled promise of a better world via the memory of the deceased crew member, who envisions a post-war world without conflict as he falls to his death. The elegant backing of Michael Kamen's piano and strings is further enhanced by a characteristically soulful tenor sax break courtesy of Raphael Ravenscroft.

"Paranoid Eyes" sees the teacher, now middle-aged and engulfed by alcoholism, grieving for the lost chances and betrayed promises of the post-war years. It's a sadly reflective piece, with a predominantly orchestral backing, followed by the more acerbic "Get Your Filthy Hands Off My Desert." The brief tirade against four world leaders—the Soviet Union's Brezhnev, Israel's Menachem Begin, the Argentine president Galtieri, and the UK's Thatcher—features Waters' heartfelt vocals against an elegant ensemble of cellos.

With a title that references his own father, in "The Fletcher Memorial Home," Roger fantasizes locking up a motley assembly of political "baddies," including Reagan, Thatcher, Brezhnev, and so on. Consigning them all to an unnamed "final solution," the vitriolic diatribe is interrupted halfway through by one of Gilmour's few meaningful solo breaks on the entire album. And the elegant ballad that follows, "Southampton Dock," is one of Waters' standout songs, centered on the image of a lonely woman at the dockside, bidding goodbye to a troopship bound for the Falklands.

Hailed by many as the finest track on the album, "The Final Cut" was originally intended as a first-person monologue by Pink in *The Wall*, but here it's a cipher for the inner struggles of a man on the brink of suicide. Roger's initially gentle vocalizing builds in emotional commitment as the string backing ebbs and flows like the tide. Not to mention Gilmour's guitar contribution, hinting at what might have been had the band gone on to tour the album—which, of course, was not to be.

Alongside "The Hero's Return," "Not Now John" is the nearest thing on the album to a hard rock number. Significantly, it's also the only track that features

OPPOSITE AND BELOW: Movie stills from *Pink Floyd: The Wall*

David Gilmour in a vocal capacity, voicing the verses while Waters takes care of the refrains and breaks. Gilmour's is the voice of the non-committed, morally feckless media man, while Roger once again occupies the principled high ground. There's a lot going on musically, with the two Chanter Sisters providing some meaty call-and-response backing vocals. It was the only track from the album to be released as a single (with "The Hero's Return" as the B-side), making it to No. 30 in the UK singles chart, and No. 7 on the Mainstream Rock Tracks (radio) chart in the US *Billboard* lists.

Compared to much of the album, at well over five minutes the closing "Two Suns in the Sunset" is something of an epic, in subject matter as much as running time. The elegiac yet simple song addresses nothing less than the prospect of nuclear Armageddon—the doomsday result of the nationalistic manifestations that Roger Waters has been railing against throughout the work. The apocalyptic imagery is made all the more effective by the support of the jazz-tinged backing of drummer Andy Newmark, and a stately fade-out from Ravenscoft's mellow saxophone.

An interesting postscript to the album's first release was the absence of "When the Tigers Broke Free," which later appeared for the first time on a CD reissue in 2004. Roger Waters had

> ## "No matter how much Waters may burn and struggle over the sad, sick world he finds himself in along with the rest of us, his diagnoses sit in a stasis of unresolved, unmoving bitterness."
>
> ### *NME*

originally intended for the song, which directly referred to his father's battlefield death in 1944, to be the opening track of *The Wall*. It was discarded on that occasion when the other three members of the band felt it was too personal, and likewise after objections from Mason and Gilmour to its inclusion on *The Final Cut*.

As if to confirm his overall responsibility for the album and its contents, Waters designed the cover himself. A simple graphic layout on a black background consisted of a

Remembrance poppy, and ribbons from various World War II medals. The interior gatefold also featured poppies, alongside military personnel and other images reflecting the musical content therein.

## Reception

With the rock music world having moved on somewhat over the previous couple of years, the music press were less sympathetic to Pink Floyd (and, specifically, Roger Waters) and their output, than on previous occasions. In the UK, while the *Melody Maker* famously called the album "a milestone in the history of awfulness," its chief competitor, the *New Musical Express*, chose to castigate Roger—recognizing it was essentially Waters' album—in particular: "No matter how much Waters may burn and struggle over the sad, sick world he finds himself in along with the rest of us, his diagnoses sit in a stasis of unresolved, unmoving bitterness." On the other side of the Atlantic, *Rolling Stone* was typically more supportive of things Floydian, calling it "essentially a Roger Waters solo album . . . a superlative achievement on several levels" and "art-rock's crowning masterpiece."

Despite it being the weakest-selling Pink Floyd album since *Meddle*, in both the United States and around the world, *The Final Cut* was awarded a Platinum disc in America, having shipped over a million copies by May 1983. And in the UK, it topped the LP charts—a position not achieved by either *The Dark Side of the Moon* or *The Wall* on their release. In the fullness of time it came to be better appreciated, but mainly as the work of Roger Waters. And historically, it heralded the eventual departure of Waters from Pink Floyd, and potentially the end of the road for the group as a creative unit.

## The Final Cut

Track Listing (original UK vinyl release)
(All songs written by Roger Waters)

### Side One
The Post War Dream
Your Possible Pasts
One of the Few
The Hero's Return
The Gunner's Dream
Paranoid Eyes

### Side Two
Get Your Filthy Hands Off My Desert
The Fletcher Memorial Home
Southampton Dock
The Final Cut
Not Now John
Two Suns in the Sunset

| | |
|---|---|
| **Recorded:** | July–December, 1982, Mayfair Studios, London; RAK Studios, London; Olympic Studios, London; EMI Abbey Road, London; Eel Pie Studios, London; Audio International, London; The Billiard Room, London; Hook End Studios, Checkendon, Oxfordshire, England |
| **Released:** | March 21, 1983 |
| **Label:** | Harvest (UK), Columbia (US) |
| **Producer:** | Roger Waters, James Guthrie, Michael Kamen |
| **Personnel:** | Roger Waters (bass guitar, guitars, synthesizers, vocals), David Gilmour (guitars, vocals), Nick Mason (drums) |

**Additional Personnel:**

Michael Kamen (piano, electric piano, harmonium), Andy Bown (Hammond organ, piano, electric piano), Ray Cooper (percussion), Andy Newmark (drums), Raphael Ravenscroft (tenor saxophone), Doreen Chanter (backing vocals), Irene Chanter (backing vocals), National Philharmonic Orchestra

**Chart Position:** US No. 6, UK No. 1, France No. 1, Italy No. 1, Germany No. 1, New Zealand No. 1, Norway No. 1, Sweden No. 1, Canada No. 2, Netherlands No. 2, Spain No. 2, Australia No. 3, Austria No. 3, Finland No. 3

LEFT: David Gilmour and his first wife, Ginger, at the movie premiere of *Pink Floyd: The Wall*, London, 1982

# a momentary lapse of reason

"I obviously had something to prove in that Roger was no longer a part of it, and obviously I had the view that people may have misunderstood or misread the way it had been with him within our history."

**David Gilmour**

OPPOSITE: Pink Floyd, now minus Roger Waters, pose backstage at the Rosemont Horizon during the band's *Momentary Lapse of Reason* tour, September 28, 1987, Rosemont, Illinois

# Solos

**F**ollowing the release of *The Final Cut*, Pink Floyd as a unit was in complete disarray. There was a general consensus in the music business—and that, of course, included the then-powerful music press—that it was, essentially, a Roger Waters solo album. And clearly the band, privately if not always in public, felt the same. The most obvious indication that the band did not regard the release as a genuine Pink Floyd collaboration was that there was no ambition on anyone's part to follow through with a supporting tour. Instead, the three remaining members after Rick Wright's departure—Waters, Gilmour, and Mason—literally went their separate ways. As Nick Mason somewhat glumly recalled: "If being part of a Roger-led Floyd meant there would be no live shows . . . and only aggravation in the recording studio, the future prospect seemed distinctly unappealing."

First out of the starting blocks with a new solo project was David Gilmour, who began recording *About Face* just months after *The Final Cut* had appeared. Co-produced with Bob Ezrin, the album had other hallmarks of recent Floyd output, including orchestral arrangements by Michael

OPPOSITE: David Gilmour poses for photographs for *The Times*, 1984

BELOW: Journalist David Sinclair interviews David Gilmour for *The Times* around the release of his second solo album, *About Face*, 1984

**"If being part of a Roger-led Floyd meant there would be no live shows . . . and only aggravation in the recording studio, the future prospect seemed distinctly unappealing."**

**Nick Mason**

Kamen, and some well-known instrumentalists such as Steve Winwood (who played Hammond organ on "Blue Light" and piano on "Love on the Air"), Jon Lord from Deep Purple on synthesizers, and percussionist Ray Cooper. All the numbers were written by Gilmour, except two co-written with Pete Townshend, "Love on the Air," and "All Lovers Are Deranged." Released in March 1984, and supported with a tour that took in dates in Europe and North America, the album did moderately well, hitting No. 21 in the UK albums chart, and No. 32 in the US *Billboard* listings. During the London dates at the Hammersmith Odeon, Nick Mason and Rick Wright turned up to join Gilmour's touring band on "Comfortably Numb" from *The Wall*.

In the fall of 1983, Rick Wright had formed Zee, a short-lived duo partnership with guitarist and keyboard player Dave Harris, who'd been with the New Romantic outfit Fashion. Their synthesizer-based album *Identity* was released in April 1984, but turned out to be an ill-judged enterprise, with Rick later describing the album as "an experimental mistake."

Roger Waters followed in late April 1984 with his first solo release, *The Pros and Cons of Hitch Hiking*. Waters had already previewed the idea to Pink Floyd—the fantasy dream of a man in mid-life crisis, having an affair with a hitch-hiker he's picked up—as an alternative option to *The Wall* in 1978, with the band choosing the latter. A strong supporting personnel was headed by Eric Clapton on lead guitar; the line-up also included co-producer Michael Kamen on piano, Andy Bown on Hammond organ, saxophonist Raphael Ravenscroft, and Andy Newmark

RIGHT: Eric Clapton (left) performs in concert with Andy Newmark (drums) and Roger Waters (center), June 16, 1984

OPPOSITE: David Gilmour, 1987

ABOVE: Nick Mason and David Gilmour, Four Seasons Hotel, Los Angeles, June 1986

on drums, all of whom had featured on previous Pink Floyd albums. Roger took a band on the road, which included Clapton, Kamen, and Newmark, with dates in the UK, Europe, and North America through June and July 1984. He toured the album in North America again in March–April 1985, with Andy Fairweather Low replacing Clapton in the line-up.

Nick Mason was the fourth of the quartet to enter the studio for a "solo" album, more accurately a joint collaboration with 10cc guitarist Rick Fenn, which was released in the summer of 1985. Almost exclusively instrumental, *Profiles* included just two vocal tracks: "Israel" sung by the UFO keyboard player Danny Peyronel, and "Lie for a Lie" which featured the renowned singer Maggie Reilly alongside David Gilmour on vocals. The album, which was mainly recorded at Britannia Row Studios, led to Mason and Fenn going on to form Bamboo Music, a production company supplying music for films and commercials.

## Disintegration and Reformation

What to many observers seemed the final disintegration of Pink Floyd had begun after Roger Waters released *The Pros and Cons of Hitch Hiking*. Waters was convinced that the band had no future, and met with manager Steve O'Rourke to discuss ongoing royalty arrangements. O'Rourke, quite correctly, felt it his duty to inform Gilmour and Mason of Waters' approach, alienating the bass player in the process. Waters then terminated his contract with O'Rourke, and informed the record companies, EMI and Columbia, that he had left the band.

When Mason and Gilmour made it clear they wished to retain O'Rourke as their manager, therefore confirming that Pink Floyd still existed as a commercial entity, Roger Waters took the radical step of applying to the High Court to prevent the name Pink Floyd being used in any capacity. When this didn't stick, after Dave Gilmour insisted it wasn't up to Waters whether the band continued to work—and following months of claims and counter claims via their lawyers—Roger returned to the High Court in December 1986 in another attempt to block the use of the group's name. He claimed the band had become a "spent force" creatively, stating that "this should be recognised in order to maintain the integrity and reputation of the group name." A spokesman for Waters went on to further explain to the press: "If the group just splits up, there's always a question of who retains rights to the name. This formal action will avoid any misunderstanding because the band Pink Floyd will then not exist."

This second attempt at preventing any use of the name Pink Floyd came to nothing, however, so while Roger worked on his next project—the soundtrack for the 1986 animated film *When the Wind Blows*—David and Nick began preparations for another album by Pink Floyd. While the legal disputes had been dragging on, Gilmour had also been gathering potential recruits for a new project, and now with Mason firmly on board, that meant the next Floyd release.

An early choice as co-producer was Bob Ezrin, who'd served the band so well during the *Wall* recordings, and was keen to join the embryonic team. Likewise, Gilmour brought in keyboard player Jon Carin, who'd been jamming with David at the latter's Hook End Studios. Regarding songwriting, David considered various individuals as possible collaborators, such as 10cc's Eric Stewart and the poet Roger McGough, before settling on composer Anthony Moore. Other notable names who participated on various tracks included the drummers Jim Keltner and Carmine Appice.

Plus of course there was keyboards man Rick Wright, who technically was ex-Pink Floyd at the time, but was hired as a paid session musician, though only making what amounted to a minor contribution to the album as a whole. But Wright's presence on the release was key in the public's perception of Pink Floyd as a viable unit, with three of its essential members still in the line-up, despite the recent upheavals, rumors, and threats of extinction.

## Realization

Recording of the new album began in November 1986, mainly at Gilmour's Astoria studio, which was housed in an elegant old houseboat moored on the River Thames. The floating studio came with its own set of problems, especially when it came to engineering the guitar sounds, as Bob Ezrin would recall: "It's not a huge environment . . . So we couldn't keep the amps in the same room with us, and we were forced to use slightly smaller amplifiers." Andy Jackson, who had worked on both the *Wall* soundtrack and *The Final Cut*, was engaged as the primary engineer on the sessions, which lasted through to March 1987.

In contrast to the previous five studio releases by Pink Floyd, which were all concept albums of one kind or another, the new collection consisted of totally separate songs. Some of the material was originally intended by David Gilmour for his third solo album, and features songs written solely by Gilmour (who delivers all the vocals), or with a number of outside songwriters.

After the opening Gilmour/Ezrin instrumental for instance,

LEFT: Nick Mason performing with Pink Floyd at Madison Square Garden, New York, October 7, 1987

the atmospheric "Signs of Life," "Learning to Fly" was penned by Gilmour, Ezrin, composer Anthony Moore, and keyboardist Jon Carin. Inspired by his love of aviation (a passion shared with Nick Mason), it's a smooth evocation of the joys of flight, sung by Gilmour, that failed to make the intended impression when released as a single just a week after the album.

Gilmour and Moore share the writing honors on two other tracks, "The Dogs of War" and "On the Turning Away." On the former, the foreboding theme is backed by the pioneer of heavy rock percussion, Carmine Appice, aided and abetted by a splintering sax solo from Scott Page. The latter is an inspiring, monumental anthem worthy of a "message" song such as this, demonstrating that Roger Waters wasn't the only Floyd member willing to wear his political heart on his sleeve.

Roxy Music guitarist Phil Manzanera was Gilmour's writing partner on "One Slip," a stark reminder of where careless actions of passion can take us, and coining the album's title phrase, a "momentary lapse of reason," into the bargain. And in Patrick Leonard, the guitarist found an effective collaborator in "Yet Another Movie," with the creation of a stark, surreal landscape worthy of the best of previous Pink Floyd collections.

Of the songs written solely by David Gilmour, the two short bursts of "A New Machine" seem as much a private call for help as a public statement. "Terminal Frost" on the other hand is a fresh mix of an old instrumental demo, with the addition of two soprano saxophones (courtesy of John Helliwell and Tom Scott) for double effect. And "Sorrow," which concludes the album, takes us from an elegiac intro, rich in distorted guitar licks, into an eight-minute song full of implied lamentations about the state of the world. Simply classic Floyd, in a knowing, latter-day context.

Significantly, the album cover art was once more assigned to the band's old design team

OPPOSITE: Roger Waters performs live onstage during his *Radio K.A.O.S.* solo tour, Met Center, Bloomington, Minnesota, September 10, 1987

ABOVE: David Gilmour live onstage with Pink Floyd, Madison Square Garden, New York, October 7, 1987

Hipgnosis, who hadn't worked on a Pink Floyd sleeve since Roger Waters' disagreement with Storm Thorgerson after *Animals* in 1977. The rift had occurred when Storm included the artwork for *Animals* in a 1978 book about Hipgnosis, *Walk Away Rene*, seemingly without the band's permission. "We didn't speak for twenty-five years," Thorgerson would recall. "That's a long time for someone I'd known since I was fourteen . . . I was upset about it for the first three or four years, and then I had to get on." The cover picture on *Momentary Lapse* featured a photographic image of a surreal flat beach landscape, on which a sea of uniform hospital beds, lined side by side, recedes into the distance. And equally noteworthy was the inside sleeve black-and-white photo of Gilmour and Mason, taken by David Bailey; Rick Wright was omitted, and his name relegated to just a mention in the credits, on account of him still not legally being a member of the band.

## Response

The public's response to the release was better than many expected, with the album climbing quickly up the American and British charts, hitting the No. 3 spot in both countries. The general feeling seemed to be that although Gilmour was clearly the prime creative force in the release, this was genuinely a Pink Floyd album. Not only because of the presence of both Mason and Wright in varying capacities, but the fact that the disparate nature of Gilmour's songs had avoided the more personal, thematic, feel of the last few Waters-driven "concept" collections. As Phil Sutcliffe put it in a review for *Q* magazine: "From this listener's point of view, despite Waters leaving in high dudgeon and Wright reappearing only in small print and on wages, *A Momentary Lapse of Reason* does sound like a Pink Floyd album." While in *Rolling Stone*, David Fricke credited much of the album's chart success to fan loyalty: "A healthy percentage of *Momentary Lapse*'s immediate sales are certainly attributable to the trust rock fans place in the brand name Pink Floyd. The album was leaping off the racks before many people had even heard a single note."

And asked a few years later whether he felt he had something to prove with the album, David Gilmour could only agree: "I obviously had something to prove in that Roger was no longer a part of it, and obviously I had the view that people may have misunderstood or misread the way it had been with him within our history. It was quite important to me to prove that there was something serious still going on there. It was 'Life after Rog,' you know."

Even before the album was finally completed, plans had been laid for the group to tour, for the first time in over six years. The first date was in Ottawa, Canada, on September 9, 1987, just a day after the North American release of the album, and two

days after it had hit the shops in the UK. The Floyd trio were augmented onstage with a seven-piece that comprised Jon Carin on keyboards, sax man Scott Page, Tim Renwick on guitar, Guy Pratt on bass guitar, percussionist Gary Wallis, and two backing vocalists.

Coincidentally, some of the dates on that first *Momentary Lapse* American tour overlapped Stateside appearances by Roger Waters, in support of his second solo album, *Radio K.A.O.S.* Like Roger's previous solo release, and the latter ones with Pink Floyd, the album was a concept project, again addressing the social ills he saw around him. Released in June '87, the record had met with decidedly muted enthusiasm from both fans and critics, and the tour—in much smaller venues than the Floyd extravaganza—was similarly low key in its appeal at the box office. Originally planned

> "Planes, beds, and pigs fly about during an extravaganza of film, animation, lights, lasers and pyrotechnics so spectacular that the aircraft overhead look like they're part of the show. My state of consciousness was straighter than the band's appearance, but this was a trip."
>
> **Simon Witter**

as a worldwide trip, the tour came to an end in late November, after just the American dates plus two concerts at Wembley Arena in London.

After three months in North America, the marathon Pink Floyd trek resumed in late January '88 with over thirty dates in New Zealand, Australia, and Japan. April and May saw them returning to North America, followed by Europe, the UK, and the US again through the summer. And in June and July of 1989, the Another Lapse tour featured more appearances in Europe, plus five concerts in the Russian capital, Moscow. Altogether the band had continued touring, off and on—with a slightly fluctuating backing line-up—for almost three years. Taking into account a one-off appearance the following year in June 1990, at Knebworth Park, just north of London, after two hundred performances the tour was estimated to have attracted over four million fans worldwide.

Throughout the tour, the band created a production that was as spectacular as any they had staged in their entire career. Over 150 riggers, electricians, and other technicians

were employed just to keep the show on the road. Describing a typical concert in New Jersey in July 1988, for the *New Musical Express*, writer Simon Witter captured the jaw-dropping impact of the event: "Despite the size of the stadium, there are no video screens, just one circular back-projection that never shows the people onstage (Pink Floyd's members are hardly riveting eye balm). Instead, the band create a spectacle of sound and vision that exploits the enormity of the venue, sucking the audience in. Planes, beds, and pigs fly about during an extravaganza of film, animation, lights, lasers and pyrotechnics so spectacular that the aircraft overhead look like they're part of the show. My state of consciousness was straighter than the band's appearance, but this was a trip."

Historically, the end of the tour marked another long hiatus in the Pink Floyd story. There was the live album culled from the trek, *Delicate Sound of Thunder*, released in November 1988, but the band's next studio album would not appear for another five and a half years, with the release of *The Division Bell* in March 1994.

ABOVE: Rick Wright, David Gilmour and Nick Mason photographed in London, May 1988

## A Momentary Lapse of Reason

Track Listing

Signs of Life (David Gilmour, Bob Ezrin)
Learning to Fly (Gilmour, Ezrin, Anthony Moore, Jon Carin)
The Dogs of War (Gilmour, Moore)
One Slip (Gilmour, Phil Manzanera)
On the Turning Away (Gilmour, Moore)
Yet Another Movie (Gilmour, Patrick Leonard)
Round and Around (Gilmour)
A New Machine (Part 1) (Gilmour)
Terminal Frost (Gilmour)
A New Machine (Part 2) (Gilmour)
Sorrow (Gilmour)

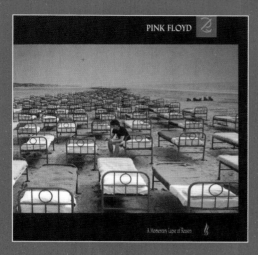

| | |
|---|---|
| **Recorded:** | November 1986 – March 1987, Astoria Studios, London; Britannia Row Studios, London; Audio International, London; Mayfair Recording Studios, London; A&M Studios, Los Angeles; the Village Recorder, Los Angeles; Can Am, Los Angeles |
| **Released:** | September 7, 1987 |
| **Label:** | EMI (UK), Columbia (US) |
| **Producer:** | Bob Ezrin, David Gilmour |
| **Personnel:** | David Gilmour (guitars, keyboards, sequencers, vocals), Nick Mason (drums, spoken vocals) |

**Additional Personnel:**
Richard Wright (piano, Hammond organ, synthesizer), Bob Ezrin (keyboards, percussion, synthesizers), Jon Carin (keyboards), Patrick Leonard (synthesizers), Bill Payne (Hammond organ), Michael Landau (guitar), Tony Levin (bass guitar, Chapman Stick), Jim Keltner (drums), Carmine Appice (drums), Steve Forman (percussion), Tom Scott (saxophones), John Helliwell [credited as John Halliwell] (saxophone), Scott Page (saxophone), Darlene Koldenhoven [credited as Darlene Koldenhavan] (backing vocals), Carmen Twillie (backing vocals), Phyllis St. James (backing vocals), Donny Gerrard (backing vocals)

**Chart Position:** US No. 3, UK No. 3, New Zealand No. 1, Australia No. 2, Netherlands No. 2, Germany No. 2, Norway No. 2, Switzerland No. 2

# the division bell

"It sounds much more like a genuine Pink Floyd record to me than anything since *Wish You Were Here.*"

**David Gilmour**

OPPOSITE: David Gilmour live onstage with Pink Floyd, Chantilly, France, July 31, 1994

# Reawakening

The intervening years since the last tour had seen relative inactivity for the trio that now constituted Pink Floyd, at least as a collective unit. On a personal level, David had been divorced, and Nick had married the TV presenter and actress Annette Lynton. And Gilmour, in particular, was prolifically involved in other artists' recording projects, both on the production and performing sides, including albums by Paul McCartney, Kate Bush, and Elton John.

Then in 1990, the two motorsport enthusiasts, Gilmour and Mason, had participated in the famous Carrera Panamericana sports car race in Mexico, at which David and manager Steve O'Rourke escaped serious injury after their car had careered off the road. A subsequent film of the race, *La Carrera Panamericana*, released in 1992, featured a soundtrack recorded by the three Floyd musicians alongside some seasoned session players—Jon Carin, Guy Pratt, Gary Wallis, and Tim Renwick—who would go on to play on the next Pink Floyd release. And in October 1992, Richard Wright, whose activities had been very low-profile since his "session man" participation in *A Momentary Lapse of Reason*, joined Gilmour and Mason at a charity gig, the Chelsea Arts Ball, at the Royal Albert Hall.

Things began to coalesce into a genuine reawakening, however, when January 1993 saw David Gilmour, Nick Mason, and Rick Wright—the latter now reunited (though still not officially) into the Floyd fold—getting together in their Britannia Row studio to start work on their next, long-awaited, album. During just a couple of weeks at the Islington studio the three, with the addition of Guy Pratt on bass guitar (who'd played with them on the *Momentary Lapse* tour), came up with

OPPOSITE: Kate Bush and David Gilmour, circa 1990

BELOW: Nick Mason pictured at home with some of the racing cars in his collection, April 10, 1990

"... as time went by, she got more and more involved with the process ... Her assistance was invaluable."

**David Gilmour**

over sixty samples of musical ideas, which they then worked on at Gilmour's studio on the houseboat *Astoria*.

There, with the aid of producer Bob Ezrin and engineer Andy Jackson, they honed the material down by a process of elimination which they referred to as "the big listen." The three band members voted on which pieces of music they preferred, awarding marks out of ten, and when it came down to the twenty-five most popular, they whittled it down again until they ended up with eleven numbers which they thought worthy of developing into an album. There was one glitch in this experiment in group democracy, however, when Rick Wright managed to award all his comrades' efforts zero points, and his own the maximum ten each. But all was settled amicably, and at the end of the day Rick actually ended up with a co-writing credit on no less than five of the eleven chosen tracks.

The other conspicuous name on the composers' list—apart from David, who appeared on ten of the eleven credits—was that of Gilmour's girlfriend, Polly Samson. Polly was a press journalist with an obvious flair for words, whose first involvement in David's songwriting was that of a supportive bystander: "In the beginning she tried not to interfere at all, and tried to encourage me to do it on my own," the guitarist admitted. "But of course that isn't the way things stay. And as time went by, she got more and more involved with the process ... Her assistance was invaluable." Samson, who David would marry soon after the release of the new album, was responsible for the lyrics of seven songs on the collection.

# High Hopes

The presence of Rick Wright as a foremost contributor, a position that had visibly diminished on the previous few albums, was confirmed with the choice of an archetypical instrumental as opener. "Cluster One" is an exercise in the sort of ambient, electronically driven music that conjures up memories of the classic Pink Floyd of old. Nevertheless, we're soon back from the depths of space rock with the first of Polly Samson's lyric collaborations with Gilmour in "What Do You Want from Me." A string of lines addressing personal self-doubt are held together with Guy Pratt's throbbing bass and Gilmour's incisive guitar and vocalizing, all layered with some rich backing voices.

Samson's second input as co-composer was a collaboration (alongside David Gilmour) with Nick Laird-Clowes, the principal songwriter for The Dream Academy, who had a 1985 hit with "Life in a Northern Town." The song, "Poles Apart," can be read (from Gilmour's perspective) as referring to both Syd Barrett and Roger Waters, but suffice to say that it makes for a powerful ballad regardless of speculation on personalized

OPPOSITE: David Gilmour and his wife, English novelist Polly Samson, pictured together in February 1999. The couple were married in 1994.

BELOW: Pink Floyd, 1993

subject matter. Samson and Laird-Clowes got together once more for "Take It Back," again with David as part of a triumvirate of lyricists. It's a strident, preachy number, with plenty of pop accessibility; perhaps not surprisingly, it became Pink Floyd's first single release in seven years, and made it to No. 23 in the UK charts.

Created while the band were assembled aboard the *Astoria* in early 1993, the second instrumental on the album, the "desert island" flavored "Marooned"—complete with the sound of seagulls and crashing waves—came out of jamming between Wright, Gilmour, and Mason. With some piano parts added by Wright at later sessions at London's Olympic Studios, the track won Best Rock Instrumental Performance at the annual Grammy Awards in 1995.

David is as overtly political as his erstwhile colleague Roger Waters in "A Great Day for Freedom." Another song with lyrics primarily from Polly Samson, it's a passionate comment on the unfulfilled dreams following the fall of the Berlin Wall in 1989. And many listeners have drawn a parallel with Gilmour's doomed relationship with Waters, despite the guitarist insisting otherwise.

On "Wearing the Inside Out," the laid-back saxophone sound of Dick Parry matches perfectly the languid lead vocals delivered effortlessly by Richard Wright. The song, with lyrics by the experimental musician Anthony Moore, was Wright's first composition for Pink Floyd since 1973 with "Us and Them," on *Dark Side of the Moon*. Sadly, it would also be Richard's last with the band.

The only track written solely by David Gilmour, the six-minute "Coming Back to Life," starts with a melancholic acoustic solo from David, before the song breaks into a loping rock number. It's a heartfelt tribute to Polly Samson, and their ongoing relationship that has, at that moment, rescued him from when he was "burned and broken." And David pulls all the synthesized stops out with "Keep Talking," in which he utilizes a sampled excerpt from a TV ad by the eminent physicist Stephen Hawking. The entire track is a perfect combination of Floydian techno-rock, call-and-response backing vocals, tough no-

RIGHT: David Gilmour performs live onstage during the *Division Bell* tour, at the Rose Bowl, Pasadena, California, April 16, 1994

nonsense drumming from Nick Mason, and down-the-line rock guitar. It was released as a single in America, where it topped the Album Rock Tracks chart (based on radio plays) in *Billboard* magazine.

Polly Samson contributes another telling lyric on the aptly titled "Lost for Words," written as part of Gilmour's response to the latest snub from Roger Waters. The guitarist had invited the band's ex-bass player and founding architect to contribute something to the album, only for Waters to answer in the negative, in no uncertain terms. The song features a suitably acerbic, Dylan-flavored vocal, including a quote of Waters' curt response containing a four-letter expletive.

And David finishes with the magnificent "High Hopes," a nostalgic recollection of the Cambridge of his youth. It's a more than powerful evocation of unrequited dreams and ambitions, from when "the grass was greener." With a church bell sounding a single note throughout, among various references to his early life and the formative background of Pink Floyd, Gilmour concludes what many went on to assume would be the final album from the band.

"High Hopes" also made reference to what would become the album's title, *The Division Bell*. Over dinner with the band one evening, Douglas Adams, the author of *The Hitchhiker's Guide to the Galaxy*, had suggested the name after hearing the song. The

bell in question summons members of the UK parliament to vote—in the words of David Gilmour, "It divides the yeses from the nos."

Once again, Pink Floyd recruited Storm Thorgerson and his design team at Hipgnosis to take care of the album's artwork. As was his usual practice, Thorgerson eschewed any reliance on what he considered photographic trickery, and instead constructed two gigantic metal heads about five meters tall. Photographed in a field in Cambridgeshire, the two heads were positioned as if talking to each other, or alternatively could be viewed as a single face—and Thorgerson went on to suggest that the third "absent" face was a reference to Syd Barrett. Storm also made the promotional film that accompanied "High Hopes," when it was released as a single in October 1994. And the film was subsequently shown during the band's *Division Bell* tour, immediately following the release of the album.

ABOVE: Launch of the custom-made Pink Floyd Skyship 600 airship promoting *The Division Bell* album, North Carolina, January 1994

PAGES 218-219: Pink Floyd live at Earls Court, London, October 1994

## Reception

The tour, which lasted a full seven months, took in over a hundred dates in North America, Mexico City, and Europe, concluding with a mammoth fifteen-concert series of shows at the Earls Court Exhibition Hall in London. Grossing an estimated hundred million dollars, and selling nearly five and a half million tickets, the tour was a huge success at every level. With a set list that began with "Astronomy Dominé" from 1967, the concerts featured high points in the band's career including songs from *Wish You Were Here* and *The Wall*, the entire *Dark Side of the Moon*, and the last two Pink Floyd albums, *A Momentary Lapse of Reason* and of course *The Division Bell*. The eight-piece accompanying ensemble consisted of instrumentalists Jon Carin, Dick Parry, Guy Pratt, Tim Renwick, and Gary Wallis (all of whom had appeared on the *Division Bell* album), plus backing vocalists Durga McBroom and Sam Brown—who were also on the recording—and Claudia Fontaine.

The public reaction to the album was as triumphant as the tour statistics, with it topping the charts in twenty territories including the US and UK. And the band themselves were more satisfied with the outcome—and obviously the sales figures—than with recent releases under the Pink Floyd banner. As David Gilmour confessed to *Mojo*, "On this album both Nick and Rick are playing all the stuff that they should be playing. Which is why it sounds much more like a genuine Pink Floyd record to me than anything since *Wish You Were Here*. It has a sort of theme about non-communication, but we're not trying to bash anybody over the head with it." And in the same interview, Rick Wright was understandably elated to be back in the thick of it: "I've written on it. I'm singing on it. I think it's

ABOVE: (top) David Gilmour, 1994

ABOVE: Pink Floyd, October 12, 1994

a much better album than the last one. It's got more of the old Floydian feel. I think we could have gone further, but we are now operating as a band. Only Nick has played the drums, and my Hammond organ is back on most tracks."

Inevitably, not all the press reviews of the album were over-ecstatic. In *Rolling Stone*, Tom Graves assessed the new collection in the context of their past releases: "Unfortunately, *A Momentary Lapse of Reason* and the live *Delicate Sound of Thunder* were only sporadically successful at achieving the stunning aural power of the Pink Floyd's previous work. Their new album, *The Division Bell*, ironically enough, seems to cry out for someone with an overriding zeal and passion—in short, a nettlesome, overbearing visionary like Roger Waters."

But as Phil Sutcliffe concluded in *Q* magazine: "*The Division Bell* should be just the job for Floydies, and a striking listen for anyone else who bumps into it. They remain unique and uniquely enigmatic. Consider how peculiarly hard it is to imagine what reactions this album would provoke, if Pink Floyd were unknown and this were their debut."

However, although Pink Floyd were certainly not a thing of the past, with their subsequent history characterized by both triumphs and tragedies, they would not—remarkably—produce a new studio album for another twenty years.

> ## "I think it's a much better album than the last one. It's got more of the old Floydian feel. I think we could have gone further, but we are now operating as a band."
> ### Rick Wright

## The Division Bell

**Track Listing**

Cluster One (David Gilmour, Richard Wright)
What Do You Want from Me (Gilmour, Wright, Polly Samson)
Poles Apart (Gilmour, Samson, Nick Laird-Clowes)
Marooned (Gilmour, Wright)
A Great Day for Freedom (Gilmour, Samson)
Wearing the Inside Out (Anthony Moore, Wright)
Take It Back (Gilmour, Samson, Laird-Clowes, Bob Ezrin)
Coming Back to Life (Gilmour)
Keep Talking (Gilmour, Samson, Wright)
Lost for Words (Gilmour, Samson)
High Hopes (Gilmour, Samson)

| | |
|---|---|
| **Recorded:** | January–December, 1993, Britannia Row Studios, London; Astoria Studios, London; EMI Abbey Road, London; Metropolis Studios, London; Creek Recording Studios, London |
| **Released:** | March 28, 1994 (UK), April 4, 1994 (US) |
| **Label:** | EMI (UK), Columbia (US) |
| **Producer:** | Bob Ezrin, David Gilmour |
| **Personnel:** | David Gilmour (guitars, bass guitar, keyboards, vocals), Nick Mason (drums, percussion), Richard Wright (piano, organ, synthesizers, vocals) |

**Additional Personnel:**
Jon Carin (piano, keyboards), Guy Pratt (bass guitar), Gary Wallis (percussion), Tim Renwick (guitars), Dick Parry (saxophone), Bob Ezrin (percussion, keyboards), Sam Brown (backing vocals), Durga McBroom (backing vocals), Carol Kenyon (backing vocals), Jackie Sheridan (backing vocals), Rebecca Leigh-White (backing vocals), Stephen Hawking (vocal samples)

**Chart Position:** US No. 1, UK No. 1, Argentina No. 1, Australia No. 1, Austria No. 1, Belgium No. 1, Canada No. 1, Chile No. 1, Denmark No. 1, Germany No. 1, Hong Kong No. 1, Ireland No. 1, Italy No. 1, Netherlands No. 1, New Zealand No. 1, Norway No. 1, Portugal No. 1, Spain No. 1, Sweden No. 1, Switzerland No. 1

# the endless river

"With Rick gone, and with him the chance of ever doing it again, it feels right that these revisited and reworked tracks should be made available as part of our repertoire."

**David Gilmour**

OPPOSITE: Rick Wright, 1996

> **"I just want to say ... I just realized the diversity of the music and everyone is different, everyone has a different approach to the music, but we've all touched people I hope ... with our music."**
>
> **Rick Wright**

## Reconciliation

Although Pink Floyd's immediate recording career seemed in some doubt, it was only seven months to the day—on May 29, 1995—after they wound up the *Division Bell* tour, that EMI put out a live collection recorded on the last leg of the trek. Entitled *Pulse*, the set featured twenty-five tracks over two CDs, and went on to top the album charts in the UK, US, and around the world. The outstanding tracks were a complete live version of *Dark Side of the Moon*, and the Syd Barrett song "Astronomy Dominé," which the band hadn't performed since the early seventies.

And at the end of 1995, there were more reminders of the Pink Floyd of old, when it was announced that the band—including founder member Syd Barrett—were being inducted into the prestigious Rock and Roll Hall of Fame. At the annual Induction Ceremony on January 17, 1996, Billy Corgan of The Smashing Pumpkins announced the induction of all five Floyd members—Gilmour, Wright, and Mason, who attended the event, plus Roger Waters and Syd Barrett, who were absent. All three present made short acceptance speeches, acknowledging the two key ex-members who were no longer part of the line-up. In David Gilmour's words: "I'll have to grab a couple more of these [awards], as two band members have started playing different tunes ... Roger and Syd, and we'll take a couple of these home for them. Thank you very much indeed."

And Rick Wright went on to namecheck Syd Barrett in particular: "He just said what I wanted to say. I wanted to say that for Roger and for Syd, particularly Syd, because the whole band started with Syd. And I just want to say that I was sitting here the whole night and I just realized the diversity of the music, and everyone is different, everyone has a different approach to the music, but we've all touched people, I hope, with our music." Following their presentation, Gilmour and Wright (with Mason declining) were joined by Billy Corgan for a near-acoustic version of "Wish You Were Here."

Later in 1996, Rick Wright saw the release of his second solo album, *Broken China*. Recorded in Wright's studio in France in the spring of 1995, it involved collaborators from Pink Floyd projects of recent years, lyricist Anthony Moore and guitarist Tim Renwick, plus on two tracks, vocalist Sinead O'Connor. It was an ambitious four-part concept album, referencing Rick's wife at the time, Millie, and her battle with depression. But, as with most solo efforts from the Floyd coterie, *Broken China* failed to make any impression sales-wise.

"... we're doing this for everyone who's not here, particularly, of course, for Syd."

**Roger Waters**

OPPOSITE: David Gilmour and Rick Wright embrace at Live 8, July 2, 2005, Hyde Park, London

ABOVE: July 2, 2005. L-R: David Gilmour, Roger Waters, Nick Mason and Rick Wright reunite for Live 8 London, a free concert in London's Hyde Park to raise awareness of the Make Poverty History campaign.

PAGES 228-229: Performing live onstage at Live 8

The prospect of some level of reconciliation between Roger Waters and the trio of Gilmour, Mason, and Wright came a little nearer fulfillment with the release of *Echoes: The Best of Pink Floyd* in November 2001. The double-CD compilation spanned the band's entire career, and co-producer James Guthrie gave the group a collective say in what tracks to select. In the event, there was not that much agreement immediately forthcoming; predictably, Waters and Gilmour were at loggerheads over various inclusions and exclusions, but eventually the four settled on a comprehensive twenty-six-track list. And there was certainly no Floyd reunion figuring in the process: "The term working collectively is a loose one!" David would tell *Mojo* magazine. "There's been the occasional phone call but no great brainstorming sessions to get us all together." When questioned about a "summit meeting" with Roger, Gilmour added: "No, Roger and I haven't spoken or been in the same room since he left in 1987."

Then, in January 2002, there was a surprise encounter between Roger Waters and Nick Mason. Nick was on holiday with his family on the Caribbean island of Mustique, when, in his own words, "I suddenly felt a forceful pair of hands grab my shoulders, and then my neck . . ." It was Roger, and the pair spent the rest of the afternoon together, then met up a couple more times during the holiday. And Nick would go on to sit in with Roger and his band when they appeared at London's Wembley Arena in June, playing on "Set the Controls for the Heart of the Sun" for the two shows, part of Waters' In the Flesh tour.

But a rapprochement between Roger Waters and his three ex-colleagues would not come until 2005, when Bob Geldof approached them with a view to playing the Live 8 benefit concert he was putting together, to raise awareness about world poverty. The concerts, staged twenty years after the 1985 Live Aid events in London and Philadelphia, and coinciding with the G8 summit of world leaders, were to be held in eleven locations around the world. When Geldof initially asked Gilmour, the guitarist declined, but then Mason, who was also approached, contacted Roger Waters. Two weeks later, Waters phoned Gilmour, and Gilmour agreed to a one-off performance. And although the band stressed that was all there was to it, there was a flurry of press excitement about a Floyd reunion.

In the event, there was no further getting together, with David Gilmour announcing in the Italian press a few months later that Pink Floyd had, indeed, disbanded. But the twenty-five minute set of just four numbers on July 2, 2005—"Breathe," "Money," "Wish You Were Here," and "Comfortably Numb"— gave the impression that the band, if calling it a day, would at least part amicably. As Roger Waters announced to the crowd in London's Hyde Park: ". . . we're doing this for everyone who's not here, particularly, of course, for Syd."

"He was such a lovely, gentle, genuine man and will be missed terribly by so many who loved him."

## "He was such a lovely, gentle, genuine man and will be missed terribly by so many who loved him."

### David Gilmour

## Tragedy

Roger's mention of Syd Barrett became all the more poignant when the reclusive co-founder of Pink Floyd died just a year later, on July 7, 2006. After his two albums, *The Madcap Laughs* and *Barrett*, both released in 1970, and the short-lived group Stars, Syd had increasingly led the life of a recluse—first in London, then back in his hometown of Cambridge. Apart from suddenly appearing at Abbey Road in 1975 during a Pink Floyd session for *Wish You Were Here* (at which the band were working on "Shine On You Crazy Diamond," a song about Barrett), Syd had very little contact with the group over the years.

All four former colleagues, however—including Gilmour, who had effectively taken Syd's place in the band—made sure he received his share of whatever royalties were forthcoming. Over the final few years of his life Barrett had been suffering from stomach ulcers and type 2 diabetes, but when he died aged sixty it was after a losing battle with pancreatic cancer.

The music world was demonstrably shocked by Syd's passing, with the *New Musical Express* publishing a special tribute edition with a picture of Barrett on the front cover. And in May 2007, a tribute concert, "Madcap's Last Laugh," was staged at London's Barbican Centre, featuring Syd's Floyd bandmates plus an all-star line-up that included Damon Albarn, Chrissie Hynde, and Kevin Ayers. At the concert Mason, Wright, and Gilmour played two Barrett songs, "Bike" and "Arnold Layne," while Roger Waters performed a version of his own song "Flickering Flame," with Jon Carin on keyboards.

Another tragedy to befall Pink Floyd came on September 15, 2008, when Rick Wright died of lung cancer, aged sixty-eight. With Wright long considered the understated member of Pink Floyd, the three survivors of the band were anxious to stress the importance of the keyboard man at every phase of their career. In 2006, Wright had become a regular participant in David Gilmour's touring band, after the guitarist released his third solo album, *On an Island*, on which Rick played Hammond organ and shared lead vocals.

Just a week after Rick's death, Gilmour played "Remember a Day"—which Wright had written for Pink Floyd's *A Saucerful of Secrets* in 1968—on the live BBC TV show *Later... with Jools*

OPPOSITE TOP: Syd Barrett pictured on his 60th birthday, January 6, 2006, Cambridge, shortly before his death in July the same year

OPPOSITE BOTTOM: Damon Albarn performing live onstage at the Syd Barrett tribute concert, May 10, 2007, Barbican, London

LEFT: Rick Wright pictured in 2006. He died September 15, 2008.

*Holland*, as a tribute to his old colleague. On the show, Gilmour said that Rick had intended to appear on the broadcast, but was not well enough. And David and Nick Mason performed the same song together at a memorial service held a few weeks later at the Notting Hill Theatre in London. At the time of his death, Rick had been working on a new solo album, which was thought to feature a series of instrumental pieces. In tribute, David Gilmour said of Rick Wright: "He was such a lovely, gentle, genuine man and will be missed terribly by so many who loved him."

And the once-seemingly irreconcilable rift between Roger Waters and David Gilmour again appeared to be a thing of the past, when the two got together on July 11, 2010, five years after their previous stage reunion at Live 8. The occasion was a charity performance in aid of the Hoping Foundation, which raised money for Palestinian children in need, held at Kidlington Hall in rural Oxfordshire. At the event, in front of an audience of just two hundred people, the pair (plus backing band) played three Floyd standbys—"Wish You Were Here," "Comfortably Numb," and "Another Brick in the Wall (Part 2)"—plus the old Phil Spector classic, "To Know Him Is to Love Him." The collaboration was clearly a one-off, but that didn't stop the *NME* raising hopes with their headline "Pink Floyd's Roger Waters and David Gilmour reunite for charity gig."

Anticipation of Pink Floyd coming together on a more regular basis was in the air once again in May 2011, when Dave Gilmour joined in on "Comfortably Numb," during Roger Waters' staging of *The Wall* at the O2 Arena in London. And also in the set, they made it the complete Floyd trio when Nick Mason joined in on tambourine for "Outside the Wall," with Gilmour on mandolin. But any closer cooperation between the three simply wasn't to be.

## Louder than Words

A positive that would come out of the loss of Richard Wright, however, was in 2012 when Gilmour and Mason decided to return to various recordings made with Wright during the *Division Bell* sessions in 1993, in order to create a new album as a tribute to the keyboard man and Floyd original. During those previous sessions, recording engineer Andy Jackson had recorded hours of ambient instrumental music, which he had tentatively dubbed *The Big Spliff*.

Now, although the Jackson project never saw the light of day, some of that material was being reconsidered by Gilmour and Mason alongside other instrumental jams and such from the 1993 recordings. With Jackson, fellow engineer Damon Iddins, and Gilmour's old friend Phil Manzanera, they set

about sorting through hours of music on board David's Astoria houseboat studio. Over six weeks the team, along with producer Martin Glover—aka Youth—put together four "movements" of predominantly instrumental music. Then in November 2013, Gilmour led sessions with Nick Mason, bass player Guy Pratt, and saxophonist Gilad Atzmon. Plus there was the addition of backing vocals on several tracks, and on the one specific vocal number—the closing "Louder than Words"—the Escala string quartet.

The album, titled *The Endless River*—a lyric borrowed from the last track of *The Division Bell*, "High Hopes"—features eighteen pieces split into the four Movements. It opens with the voice of Rick Wright conversing with Gilmour on "Things Left Unsaid," a splendidly atmospheric piece that draws us into the synth-and-organ ambience of classic Pink Floyd. Rick Wright is suitably dominant on "It's What We Do," until Gilmour takes over with a shimmering guitar solo, before closing the first section with the appropriately titled two minutes of "Ebb and Flow." Rick leads again into the second Movement, with "Sum" relying more on Nick Mason's heavy percussion, before "Skins" gives us an almost swing-era demonstration of the drummer's instrumental prowess. After some hypnotic repetition on "Unsung," the Movement concludes with "Anisina," a forceful, anthemic piece with a standout sax break courtesy of Gilad Atzmon.

"The Lost Art of Conversation," which opens Movement number three, has Rick playing a conventional piano over the swirling sounds of synths, before we're taking a trip down the more jaunty "On Noodle Street." "Night Light" takes us back into the cosmic territory of bygone Floyd space opera, before the oddly titled "Allons-y (1)" gives a full orchestral feel to things. Then we find ourselves in the cathedral-like echo chamber that was Rick Wright on the Albert Hall pipe organ in "Autumn '68," before "Allons-y (2)" preludes "Talkin' Hawkin'," with another sample of Professor Stephen Hawking as heard on *The Division Bell*'s "Keep Talking." "Calling" opens the final Movement of the work, co-written by experimentalist Anthony Moore, who'd contributed as lyricist on the previous Floyd album. "Eyes to Pearls" is something of a laid-back interlude before "Surfacing," a typical Floydian panorama of electronic sound.

And for the finale of *Endless River*, we have Gilmour delivering the only vocal on the album, "Louder than Words." The lyrics were the work of Polly Samson, an emotive plea for understanding, all the more pertinent in the context of the band's history. As her husband, David Gilmour, would spell out as the *raison d'etre* of the album: "With Rick gone, and with him the chance of ever doing it again, it feels right that these revisited and reworked tracks should be made available as part of our repertoire."

The cover picture on the album was a collaborative work on the part of Hipgnosis co-founder Aubrey Powell. His partner in the design company, Storm Thorgerson—who had designed over twenty sleeves for Pink Floyd, including compilations and live albums—had passed away in 2013, after a long struggle with cancer. Powell chose the photographic work of an eighteen-year-old Egyptian artist, Ahmed Emad Eldin, whose illustration depicted a young man in a small boat punting across a sea of clouds.

Released on November 7, 2014, the album was greeted with mixed feelings by reviewers, with some, like *The Guardian*'s Alexis Petridis, striking a note of skepticism, if not outright cynicism: "The official line is that it's intended as a belated tribute to Richard Wright, the keyboard player who died of cancer in 2008. A conspiracy theorist might suggest it's one final act of niggly passive

OPPOSITE: Roger Waters performs live onstage during his The Wall Live tour, O2 Arena, London, May 11, 2011. The tour ran until September 21, 2013.

aggression, ensuring the band's own final act doesn't involve their former bassist." Nevertheless, the Floyd public entertained no such reservations, with the album debuting at No. 1 in the UK chart, and No. 3 in America. In just the two months until the end of the year, *The Endless River* had sold over 2.5 million copies worldwide.

## Rise Up!

As seemed the intention from the start of the project, *The Endless River* was considered by Mason and Gilmour to be the last Pink Floyd gesture as an active unit. Even a support tour for the album seemed inappropriate, as the release was as much about Rick Wright as the guitarist and drummer. Gilmour was adamant that the band had indeed ceased operating, as he stressed in an interview with *Classic Rock* magazine in 2015: "I'm done with it. I've had 48 years in Pink Floyd—quite a few of those years at the beginning, with Roger. And those years in what is now considered to be our heyday were 95% musically fulfilling and joyous and full of fun and laughter. I certainly don't want to let the other 5% colour my view of what was a long and fantastic time together. But it has run its course, we are done—and it would be fakery to go back and do it again."

But although the band as such was no more, there was considerable activity on the Floyd front over the next few years.

OPPOSITE: Nick Mason's band Saucerful of Secrets perform live at the Edinburgh Usher Hall, Scotland, May 4, 2022. The band formed in 2018 to perform the early music of Pink Floyd and comprises Nick Mason, bassist Guy Pratt, guitarists Gary Kemp and Lee Harris, and keyboardist Dom Beken.

ABOVE: David Gilmour performs in concert at Circo Massimo, Rome, Italy, July 2, 2016

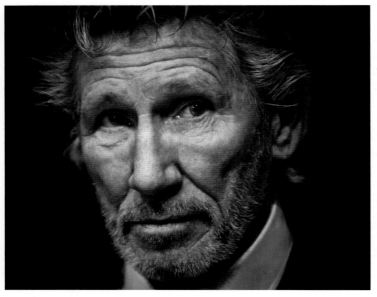

**"I'm done with it. I've had 48 years in Pink Floyd—quite a few of those years at the beginning, with Roger. And those years in what is now considered to be our heyday were 95% musically fulfilling and joyous and full of fun and laughter."**

**David Gilmour**

Amid a flurry of post-Floyd album releases, in November 2016 there came *The Early Years 1965–1972*, made up of outtakes, live tracks, and remixes, followed in 2019 by *The Later Years*, covering the post-Waters period.

Various other live albums and box sets appeared, and in 2018 Nick Mason put together his band Nick Mason's Saucerful of Secrets. As the name suggested, the unit—comprised of Mason plus bassist Guy Pratt, ex-Spandau Ballet guitarist Gary Kemp, Lee Harris (formerly with Ian Dury's Blockheads) also on guitar, and Dom Beken on keyboards—concentrated on early Pink Floyd material. After debuting in London, a 2018 European tour was followed by a North American trek in 2019—during which, at New York's Beacon Theatre, Roger Waters joined the band to sing "Set the Controls for the Heart of the Sun." At the time of writing, the band still get together sporadically, and in 2020 released the album *Live at the Roundhouse*.

Then in February 2022, the world was shaken by the news of the Russian invasion of Ukraine. Gilmour and Mason immediately got together, and under the name of Pink Floyd recorded a single, "Hey, Hey, Rise Up!" in protest at the invasion, with the proceeds going to the Ukrainian Humanitarian Relief Fund. The single, which featured the Ukrainian singer Andriy Khlyvnyuk, plus Guy Pratt and Nitin Sawhney on bass and keyboards, respectively, was released on April 8, 2022, with a reworked version of "A Great Day for Freedom" from *The Division Bell* on the B-side.

The circumstances surrounding the release, however,

had already become another bone of contention between Roger Waters and his former colleagues. As Pink Floyd, Mason and Gilmour had removed the band's music from streaming services in Russia and its ally Belarus, but it transpired that the band's material recorded with Waters remained, leading to the conclusion that Roger must have blocked the removal. Interviewed in *The Guardian*, David Gilmour was guarded in the outright condemnation of his old bandmate: "Let's just say I was disappointed and let's move on. Read into that what you will."

So the saga of Gilmour versus Waters, as a sub-plot to the history of Pink Floyd, continues seemingly off-and-on forever. But the legacy of that history, which stretches back over fifty years, is unique in the annals of rock music. Whether the surviving members collaborate again, and in whatever combination, seems irrelevant compared to the incalculable impact that the music of Pink Floyd has made over the years.

OPPOSITE: Roger Waters, 2016 (top); David Gilmour, 2016 (center); Nick Mason, 2014 (bottom)

# The Endless River

Track Listing

### 1st Movement
Things Left Unsaid (David Gilmour, Richard Wright)
It's What We Do (Gilmour, Wright)
Ebb and Flow (Gilmour, Wright)

### 2nd Movement
Sum (Gilmour, Wright, Nick Mason)
Skins (Gilmour, Wright, Mason)
Unsung (Wright)
Anisina (Gilmour)

### 3rd Movement
The Lost Art of Conversation (Wright)
On Noodle Street (Gilmour, Wright)
Night Light (Gilmour, Wright)
Allons-y (1) (Gilmour)
Autumn '68 (Wright)
Allons-y (2) (Gilmour)
Talkin' Hawkin' (Gilmour, Wright)

### 4th Movement
Calling (Gilmour, Anthony Moore)
Eyes to Pearls (Gilmour)
Surfacing (Gilmour)
Louder than Words (Gilmour, Polly Samson)

**Recorded:** June 1969, Royal Albert Hall, London; 1993–1994, Britannia Row Studios, London; Astoria Studios, London; Olympic Studios, London; 2013–2014, Astoria Studios, London; Medina Studios, Hove, UK
**Released:** November 7, 2014

**Label:** Parlophone (UK), Columbia (US)
**Producer:** David Gilmour, Youth (Martin Glover), Andy Jackson, Phil Manzanera, Bob Ezrin (co-producer)
**Personnel:** David Gilmour (guitars, keyboards, Hammond organ, percussion, bass guitar, vocals), Nick Mason (drums, percussion), Richard Wright (Hammond organ, Farfisa organ, synthesizers, Royal Albert Hall organ, keyboards, vocals)
**Additional Personnel:** Jon Carin (synthesizers), Guy Pratt (bass guitar), Bob Ezrin (bass guitar, keyboards), Andy Jackson (bass guitar), Damon Iddins (keyboards), Anthony Moore (keyboards), Gilad Atzmon (tenor saxophone, clarinet), Durga McBroom (backing vocals), Louise Marshall (backing vocals), Sarah Brown (backing vocals), Youth (synthesizers, keyboards), Eddie Bander (synthesizers, keyboards), Michael Rendall (synthesizers, keyboards)
**Escala:** Chantal Leverton (viola), Victoria Lyon (violin), Honor Watson (violin), Helen Nash (cello)

**Chart Position:** US No. 3, UK No. 1, Austria No. 1, Belgium No. 1, Canada No. 1, Croatia No. 1, Czech Republic No. 1, Denmark No. 1, France No. 1, Germany No. 1, Greece No. 1, Ireland No. 1, Israel No. 1, Italy No. 1, Netherlands No. 1, New Zealand No. 1, Norway No. 1, Poland No. 1, Portugal No. 1, Sweden No. 1, Switzerland No. 1

# picture credits

T: Top; B: Bottom; L: Left; R: Right; C: Center

**ALAMY: P8L, P216-217, P218-219** Lenscap **P9** MediaPunch Inc **P10** Album/Alamy Stock Photo **P12-13, P53** Tony Byers **P14** Tony Gale **P21, P37, P86R** Pictorial Press Ltd **P29, P33, P45, P50, P54, P57, P67, P83, P99, P111, P127, P143, P159** Vinyls/Alamy Stock Photo **P38** Odile Noël **P46** Roger Tillberg **P49** Brian Shuel/Redferns **P55, P100, P103, P107** Everett Collection Inc **P70** Masheter Movie Archive **P74-75, P76, P77T, P77B, P136-137, P137** Philippe Gras **P86L** Edward Roth **P96-97, P164, P221** dcphoto **P108** Trinity Mirror/Mirrorpix **P110, P120-121, P124, P126** Gijsbert Hanekroot **P114-115, P128, P213** ilpo musto **P132T, P132B, P181** Rajko Simunovic **P138** Lebrecht Music & Arts **P141** Edward Roth **P166** Contraband Collection **P189** Popimages **P194** Ross Marino/Rock Negatives/MediaPunch **P224** DaniFoto **P227** Antonio Pagano **P231** Associated Press **P236-237** Alan Rennie/Alamy Live News **P238C** Rich Fury/Invision/AP **P238B** Drew Gurian/Invision/AP **GETTY: COVER, P16, P32, P42, P44, P125, P171L** Michael Ochs Archives **P2, P176-177, P178-179, P180, P184-185** Pete Still **P6** King Collection/Avalon **P8R, P18L, P18R, P19, P31, P34** Andrew Whittuck/Redferns **P11** Brian Aris/Live 8 **P17, P20, P22-23, P25, P26R, P27** Adam Ritchie/Redferns **P24, P144** Keystone/Hulton Archive **P26L, P52** GAB Archive/Redferns **P28** Chris Morris/PYMCA/Avalon **P30** Doug McKenzie **P36** John Rodgers/Redferns **P39** Ivan Keeman/Redferns **P40-41** Arthur Sidey/Daily Mirror/Mirrorpix **P43, P133** Chris Walter/WireImage **P48-49, P50-51, P58, P66, P91, P220T** Blick/RDB/ullstein bild **P56, P71** Movie Poster Image Art **P60** Nick Hale/Hulton Archive **P61** Gems/Redferns **P62** George Wilkes/Hulton Archive **P64** Ron Howard/Popperfoto **P65** Chris Morphet **P68, P117, P118-119, P120-121, P122, P163, P206-207** Michael Putland **P72** Screen Archives **P73** Bettmann **P78-79** Hans-Jurgen Dibbert - K & K/Redferns **P80, P84** Mike Randolph/Paul Popper/Popperfoto **P81** Brian Shuel/Redferns **P82, P92-93, P94-95, P112, P171R** Koh Hasebe/Shinko Music **P87, P116** Gijsbert Hanekroot/Redferns **P88-89** Jorgen Angel/Redferns **P89, P168** Evening Standard/Hulton Archive **P90, P98** Bernard Allemane/INA **P102** Icon and Image **P130-131** Smith Collection/Gado **P134-135** Nik Wheeler/Sygma **P139** David Warner Ellis/Redferns **P142** Richard E. Aaron/Redferns **P147, P165** Watal Asanuma/Shinko Music **P148** Ian Dickson/Redferns **P150-151** Daniel SIMON/Gamma-Rapho **P152-153, P155** David Redfern/Redferns **P154, P160, P173, P174-175, P222** Rob Verhorst/Redferns **P156, P196, P197** Erica Echenberg/Redferns **P157, P174** Donaldson Collection **P158** David Tan/Shinko Music **P162, P201** Jeffrey Mayer/WireImage **P169** Jim McCrary/Redferns **P175** Adam Berry/Redferns **P182, P211** Dave Hogan/Hulton Archive **P186, P204** Gary Gershoff **P187L** Peter Noble/Redferns **P187R** Roger Ressmeyer/Corbis/VCG **P198-199** Vinnie Zuffante **P200-201** Armando Gallo **P202-203** Ebet Roberts/Redferns **P205** Jim Steinfeldt/Michael Ochs Archives **P208** Chip HIRES/Gamma-Rapho **P210** Peter Macdiarmid **P212** Dave Benett **P214-215** Lester Cohen **P217-218** Vinnie Zuffante/Stringer **P220B** Avalon **P225** Ron Galella, Ltd./Ron Galella Collection **P226** MJ Kim **P228-229** Mick Hutson/Redferns **P230B, P234-235** Marc Broussely/Redferns **P232-233** Dave M. Benett/CI Getty Images Entertainment **P233** Brian Rasic **P237** Roberto Panucci/Corbis **P238T** Simone Cecchetti/Corbis **SHUTTERSTOCK: P104-105, P106, P109** Bayerische Rundfunk/Ortf/Kobal **P146** Ian Dickson **P149** Jonathan Hordle **P172, P188, P190, P191** Mgm/Ua/Kobal **P192** Richard Young **P230T** Geoff Robinson

# sources

## Magazines and newspapers

*Beat Instrumental, Billboard, Circus, Classic Rock, Disc and Music Echo, Goldmine, Guitar World, International Times, Let It Rock, Los Angeles Times, Melody Maker, Mojo, Musician, New Musical Express, Newsweek, Phonograph Record, Q Magazine, Rolling Stone, Sounds, The Daily Telegraph, The Guardian, The Sun, The Times, The Village Voice, Uncut*

## TV, Radio and Websites

All Pink Floyd Fan Network (website closed), bbc.co.uk/music/uk, brain-damage.co.uk, floydianslip.com, KPPC-FM radio, *Omnibus* (BBC TV), *The Pink Floyd Story* (Capital Radio) *The Source* radio *Top Gear* (BBC Radio), ukrockfestivals.com

## Books

Blake, Mark *Pigs Might Fly* Aurum Press, 2007

Boyd, Joe *White Bicycles: Making Music in the 1960s* Serpent's Tail, 2006

Butterworth, Richard *On Track... Pink Floyd* Sonicbond Publishing, 2022

Heylin, Clinton *It's One for the Money* Constable, 2015

Manning, Toby *The Rough Guide to Pink Floyd* Rough Guides, 2006

Mason, Nick *Inside Out: A Personal History of Pink Floyd* Weidenfeld & Nicholson, 2004

Miles, Barry *Hippie* Cassell Illustrated, 2003

Miles, Barry *London Calling: A Countercultural History of London since 1945* Atlantic Books, 2010

Miles, Barry *Pink Floyd: A Visual Documentary* Omnibus, 1981

Miles, Barry *The Greatest Album Covers of All Time* Collins & Brown, 2005

Moller, Karen *Technicolor Dreamin': The 1960's Rainbow and Beyond* Trafford Publishing, 2006

Povey, Glenn *Echoes: The Complete History of Pink Floyd* 3C Publishing, 2008

Schaffner, Nicholas *Saucerful of Secrets: The Pink Floyd Odyssey* Sidgwick & Jackson, 1991

Thorgerson, Storm *Mind Over Matter: The Images of Pink Floyd* Omnibus Press, 2015

Watkinson, Mike; Anderson, Pete *Crazy Diamond: Syd Barrett & the Dawn of Pink Floyd* Omnibus, 2001